How to Democratize Europe

HOW TO DEMOCRATIZE EUROPE

Stéphanie Hennette

Thomas Piketty

Guillaume Sacriste

Antoine Vauchez

Harvard University Press

Cambridge, Massachusetts
London, England
2019

First printing

The Introduction, Chapters 2, 3, 4, 5, 6, and the Glossary were originally published in French as *Pour un traité de démocratisation del'Europe,* © Editions du Seuil, 2017.

Chapter 16 was originally published in French as Stéphanie Hennette, Thomas Piketty, Guillaume Sacriste, and Antoine Vauchez, "Pour un traité de démocratisation de l'Europe. Pourquoi ? Comment?" in *Do You Law? Politique, Justice, Libertés. Libération,* April 13, 2017.

Chapter 17 was originally published as Stéphanie Hennette-Vauchez, Thomas Piketty, Guillaume Sacriste, and Antoine Vauchez, "European parliamentary sovereignty on the shoulders of national parliamentary sovereignties: A Reply to Sébastien Platon" in *Verfassungsblog,* March 3, 2017.

Chapter 18 was originally published as Stéphanie Hennette, Thomas Piketty, Guillaume Sacriste and Antoine Vauchez, "Politicizing Europe, Europeanizing Politics" in *Books & Ideas,* October 5, 2017.

Chapter 19 reprints text posted at tdem.edu as Manifesto for the Democratization of Europe, a project coordinated by a group composed of Manon Bouju, Lucas Chancel, Anne-Laure Delatte, Stéphanie Hennette, Thomas Piketty, Guillaume Sacriste, and Antoine Vauchez.

Library of Congress Cataloging-in-Publication Data

Names: Hennette-Vauchez, Stéphanie, author. | Piketty, Thomas, 1971- author. | Sacriste, Guillaume, 1972- author. | Vauchez, Antoine, author.
Title: How to democratize Europe / Stephanie Hennette, Thomas Piketty, Guillaume Sacriste, Antoine Vauchez.
Other titles: Pour un traité de démocratisation de l'Europe. English
Description: Cambridge, Massachusetts : Harvard University Press, 2019. | Includes index.
Identifiers: LCCN 2019000529 | ISBN 9780674988088 (alk. paper)
Subjects: LCSH: Democratization—European Union countries. | Democracy—European Union countries. | European Union countries— Politics and government—21st century. | European Union countries— Economic policy. | Populism—Europe. | Equality—Europe. | Right-wing extremists—Europe.
Classification: LCC JN40 .H4613 2019 | DDC 320.94—dc23 LC record available at https://lccn.loc.gov/2019000529

– *Contents* –

Born in the urgency of a French presidential campaign, presented and discussed in the midst of a rich European election year that saw a succession of elections in the three principal economies of the eurozone—in France (May 2017), Germany (September 2017), and Italy (March 2018)—the proposed international Treaty on the Democratization of the Governance of the Euro Area, or "T-Dem," has been the subject of a lively and rich debate since its appearance. It must be said that the terrain of the reform of the European Union is in every way a field of land mines, above all for those who seek—as we have sought in the framework of the T-Dem—to surpass the ritual opposition of "sovereigntist" and "federalist" viewpoints. Because the T-Dem was quickly translated into German, Catalan, Italian, Greek, Dutch, Portuguese, Serbian, and Turkish, it has been possible to discuss the proposal in a multiplicity of political meetings, academic conferences, blogs, and journals at the national as well as at the European level. This is indeed what we wanted in seeking to get the debate on the future of Europe out of the technocratic ruts into which it has too often fallen.

This book aims to partly restore these exchanges. In this sense, this volume is much more than a simple English version of the treaty—which, it is true, was still lacking. Enriched by a historical perspective on the conditions of the emergence of the eurozone, it also includes a very diverse array of contributions and reactions presented by academics (jurists, political scientists, economists) and politicians (German,

Belgian, French, Greek, Dutch, and Portuguese). Far from being panegyrics, the contributions—however brief—are focused on the project, investigate its democratic potential, question its feasibility, and propose possible future adjustments.

It will be said that much has changed since the T-Dem first appeared. Certain political givens presented in the book—beginning with the balance of progressive and conservative forces (see Table 2, p. 55)—have now been surpassed, and groups such as the political Left in France, Germany, and Italy are paying the price for their inability to change the course of the European project. But even if the political framework has assuredly been transformed, the diagnosis of the autocratic inclination of the government of the eurozone still holds. Witness the opaque conditions in which the renewal of the Board of Directors of the European Central Bank led to the appointment of a former director of Lehman Brothers as vice president;[1] or the litany of reports, notes, and other proposals for reform that soon enough relegated to the back burner the democratic reform (which Emmanuel Macron at one time timidly put forth), to the benefit of a consolidation of the technocratic structure of the government of the eurozone. As if the fragile European economic recovery was enough to make one forget the profound democratic crisis the European project is going through.

The T-Dem will appear to some more "utopian" than ever. Sure. For if it is a utopia, it is a *concrete* utopia," in the sense that the late Erik Olin Wright gave this expression:[2] a project that, in revealing another European possibility, casts a harsh light on the gap that exists between the "big words" of European democracy ("democratic government," "accountability," and so on) and the reality of the practices of the eurozone government. It is also a project that, in seeking to surpass the partitioning of disciplines that so often prevails in reflections on the European question, must stimulate not only the imagination but also active reforms—by showing, against the idea that European treaties would bring about a space of *impossibility*, that there is in fact some play and margin for a political refounding. Moreover, while this proposal might appear utopian in "cold" times, when governments don't feel pressured to reform institutions and policies, it might be the only realistic way forward in the "heated" times of financial and economic crises, when the technocratic injunctions of Eurogroup networks of financial ministers and treasuries collide with newly elected, democratic governments.

Finally, this project is conceived as a work in progress. It is open to revisions, corrections, and additions. Without reviving the distant horizons of abstract utopias that have done so much harm to the credibility of the European project, the T-Dem makes it possible to leave behind the indignation and lamentation that too often monopolize discussions of the European project and to reflect on the practical conditions (political, legal, and such) of its realization. The workshop on democratization regarding the T-Dem project that was open from September 2017 to April 2018 brought together, in thematic sections, students, scholars, NGO activists, and political leaders to reflect very concretely on possible inflections and extensions of the T-Dem.

Our intention in the coming months and years, particularly in the perspective of the upcoming European elections and the subsequent terms of office at the European Commission and the European Central Bank, is obviously to contribute to the enrichment of this proposal, on the basis of these discussions and exchanges. It is not certain, for example, that the reforming ambition needs to be limited to the eurozone alone: with the expanding scope of the "European Semester" surveillance scheme across the policy spectrum (from structural reforms of labor markets and pensions to issues of competitiveness of national judicial systems, public administration reform, and so on), the eurozone government has become to a large extent EU government *tout court*. In this sense, it is more adapted to speak straightaway of the creation of a true "European Assembly" whose vocation would be to welcome all the countries who want to join it (and not an "Assembly of the Euro Area"). Likewise, it would probably be useful to place ourselves immediately at a more ambitious level in terms of fiscal and social justice and the capacity to invest in the future, by granting this European Assembly the power to enact a common tax on the highest revenues and patrimonies (which are the primary beneficiaries of economic integration), and not just a common tax on the profits of the societies.

All of these questions have led us to draft a revised proposal entitled the "Manifesto for the Democratization of Europe" (see Chapter 19), which was backed by more than 120 intellectuals, activists, and politicians from all over Europe, published on December 10, 2018, in eight European newspapers, and presented for signatures from all European citizens (www.tdem.eu). The Manifesto puts on the table a concrete plan to democratize European institutions and policies. It complements the

Democratization Treaty with a full-fledged budget, grounded on long-term investments in public goods of European scale (ecological transition, research and universities, welcoming of migrants, and so on), financed by the fiscal solidarity of those (top incomes, highest wealth owners, biggest polluters, GAFA) who have benefited the most from the creation of the Single Market and globalization processes.

For whatever conservatives say, the European treaties will continue to be changed and rewritten, with the risk that this entails new circumventions of democracy. Rather than wait for the next crisis and the usual last-minute makeshifts, it is better to prepare now for these discussions and to openly debate democratic alternatives and precise proposals in the full light of day. All things considered, our sole ambition is to contribute to ensuring that this debate on the democratization of Europe never stops.

—Translated by Marc LePain

Notes

1. See the Manifesto published in Le Monde on the 28th of January 2018 : "Democratizing Europe Starts with the Nominations of the ECB", available in English at : http://piketty.blog.lemonde.fr/2018/01/29/democratising-europe-begins-with-ecb-nominations/ (last visited 4th February 2019).
2. Erik Olin Wright, *Envisioning Real Utopias* (Verso, 2010).

– *Abbreviations* –

AGS	*Annual Growth Survey*
AMR	*Alert Mechanism Report*
BEPGs	Broad Economic Policy Guidelines
CJEU	Court of Justice of the European Union
COREPER	Conseil des Representants Permanents (Committee of Permanent Representatives)
CSRs	*Country-Specific Reports* but also *Country-Specific Recommendations*
DG	Directorate-General
DG ECFIN	Directorate-General for Economic and Financial Affairs
ECB	European Central Bank
ECOFIN	Economic and Financial Affairs Council
EDP	Excessive Deficit Procedure
EES	European Employment Strategy
EFC	Economic and Financial Committee
EMS	European Monetary System
EMU	Economic and Monetary Union
EPP	European People's Party
ESM	European Stability Mechanism
EWG	Eurogroup Working Group
GCC	German Constitutional Court
IDR	*In-Depth Review*
IGC	Intergovernmental Conference
IMF	International Monetary Fund

LABREF   Labor Market Reforms Database
LIME   Lisbon Methodology
MIP   Macroeconomic Imbalance Procedure
MoU   memorandum of understanding
TEU   Treaty on European Union
TFEU   Treaty on the Functioning of the European Union
TSCG   Treaty on Stability, Coordination and Governance

– *Introduction* –

Over the past ten years of economic and financial crisis, a new center of European power has taken shape: the "government" of the euro area. The expression may seem badly chosen, as it is difficult to identify the democratically accountable "institution" that today implements European economic policies. We are aiming at a moving and blurred target. Characterized by its informality and opacity, the central institution of that government—the Eurogroup, composed of finance ministers, an ECB board member, and a European commissioner—operates outside the framework of European treaties and is in no way accountable to either the European Parliament or national parliaments. Worse, the institutions that form the backbone of that government—from the European Central Bank (ECB) and the European Commission to the Eurogroup and the European Council—operate in combinations that constantly vary from one policy to the next (whether in issuing Troika memorandums, European Semester budgetary, economic, and fiscal "recommendations," or bank "evaluations" under the Banking Union).

However scattered they may be, these different policies are truly "governed," as a hard core has emerged from the ever closer union of national and European economic and financial bureaucracies—notably the French and German national treasuries, the ECB executive board, and the European Commission. As matters stand, this is where the euro area is supposedly governed from and where the proper political tasks of coordination, mediation, and balancing among the current economic and social interests are carried out. When in 2012 François Hollande gave up reforming the Treaty on Stability, Coordination and Governance, a cornerstone of this euro-area governance, he contributed to consolidating this new power structure. From then onward, this European executive structure has only seen its competences expand. Over a decade, its scope for intervention has become significant, ranging from "budgetary consolidation" (austerity) policies to far-reaching coordination of national economic policies (authorized by six legislative measures and then another two, usually called the "Six-Pack" and the "Two-Pack"), the setup of rescue plans for member states facing financial distress (via memorandums and Troika), and the supervision of all private banks.

Both mighty and elusive, the government of the euro area evolved in a blind spot of political controls, in a sort of democratic black hole. Who, indeed, controls the drafting process of memorandums of understanding, which impose significant structural reforms in return for the financial assistance of the European Stability Mechanism? Who scrutinizes the executive operations of the institutions making up the Troika? Who monitors the decisions taken within the European Council of the heads of state or government of the euro area? Who knows exactly what is negotiated within the two core committees of the Eurogroup—the Economic Policy Committee and the Economic and Financial Committee? Neither national parliaments, which at best simply control their own executive, nor the European Parliament, which has carefully been sidelined from euro-area governance. In view of the euro-area government's opacity and isolation, the many criticisms voiced against it seem well deserved, starting with Jürgen Habermas's denunciation of a "post-democratic autocracy."

While considering this democratic black hole, it is critical to keep in mind that the problem it is not just a matter of principle, nor is it merely an issue of checks and balances. It has a real impact on the very substance of the economic policies carried out in the euro area. It leads to a form of generalized indifference toward whistleblowers and other discordant voices—as is best exemplified today vis-à-vis the quasi-unanimous chorus of economists emphasizing the inevitability of a renegotiation of Greece's debt. It favors a significant lack of responsiveness to the very pointed signals sent by national electoral processes, which persistently feature the rise of far-right populism. From a more substantive point of view, this power structure overstates the stakes associated with financial stability and market confidence, and downplays the issues that are the most relevant for the majority (employment, growth, fiscal convergence, social cohesion, and solidarity) and that only come to the fore with great difficulty.

There is, therefore, an urgent need to upgrade democratic values and place representative politics at the core of European economic policies. It is high time to get rid of this new European power's opacity and lack of political accountability—by inserting a democratically elected institution at its heart. Only a Parliamentary Assembly would have the sufficient legitimacy to hold this euro-area government politically accountable. Some will argue that strengthening the position of the European Parliament may here suffice, but things are not (or at least are no longer) that simple. Governing the euro area is not like governing Europe in the past: it is no longer about organizing a common market, it is now about coordinating economic policies, harmonizing tax systems, and fostering convergence among national budgetary policies, thereby entering the very heart of member states' social contracts. It would thus be difficult not to involve national parliaments directly, unless they are to be progressively stripped of their main constitutional powers and the institutions of national democracy are to be left to run idle. Because they remain closely connected to political life in the individual member states, national parliaments are the sole institutions with sufficient legitimacy to democratize this mighty intergovernmental network of bureaucracies that has emerged over the past decade. This, moreover, echoes the proposal Joschka Fischer made in his speech at Humboldt University on May 12, 2000 (and more recently in his *Europeanizing Europe* op-ed on October 27, 2011), when he argued that the creation of a European chamber composed of representatives from national parliament would be the crucial step toward political union.

But this Assembly would need to be entrusted with the necessary resources to effectively counterbalance the present governing structure, whose influence derives, not only from the institutional prerogatives it has accumulated over a decade, but first and foremost from its ability to expertly define the scope of any potential policies. In order to avoid a rump Parliament, constantly faced with a *fait accompli,* or one that merely rubber-stamps diagnoses or decisions made elsewhere, this Assembly must be given the capacities to fully participate in managing the euro area. This implies that it must be able to weigh in effectively on the political agenda: by co-producing the agenda of Euro Summit meetings and the biannual work program of the Eurogroup, and also by exercising the power of legislative initiative—which the European Parliament lacks so far, rendering it unable to choose its own battles. It also implies that this Assembly will be able to step in at every crucial juncture of the governance process of the euro area, whether under the European Semester (and the related "excessive budgetary procedure"), the financial conditionality included in memorandums of understanding, or the selection of the main executive leaders of the euro area. Finally, this requires providing the Assembly with its own autonomous and pluralist staff of experts, as well as investigative powers that would apply to all institutions constituting the new government.

Under this treaty democratizing the euro area, member states would thus be delegating to the Assembly the power to vote on and set the base rate of corporation tax and a common tax rate to finance the euro-area budget. The member states would remain able to vote on any additional tax rate applicable to the same base. The Assembly would also be empowered to enact across the euro area the automatic exchange of bank details, and to pursue a concerted policy for restoring progressive income and wealth taxes, while jointly and actively combatting external tax havens. Europe must be able, while participating in globalization, to control vital matters of tax justice and political voluntarism in the regulation of globalization: these proposals will achieve substantial and tangible progress in that direction.

The treaty would also allow legislative action to mutualize public debt over 60% of each member state's GDP. Such debt-mutualization would enable the adoption of a common interest rate and the promulgation of a partial or total debt moratorium, in conjunction with the ECB. This proposal echoes that of a European Redemption Fund made in 2011 by the German Council of Economic Experts, while adding a political dimension to it. Only a democratic body—namely, the Parliamentary Assembly of the Euro Area—would be entitled to fix yearly investment and deficit levels, on the basis *inter alia* of the economic and social conditions pertaining within the euro area.

Of course, there is no institutional panacea. No institutional reform, however well thought out, can work miracles. Everyone is conscious that a new body will not by itself change Europe's political destiny. Ultimately, a thorough review of the European project will become unavoidable. But as we move along this path, setting up a Parliamentary

Assembly for the Euro Area stands as code for a wider political and cultural fight for the democratization of the European project and for a new direction for the policies carried out on its behalf.

As the T-Dem shows, it is possible to act swiftly, without necessarily going through a highly cumbersome process of revising treaties involving all twenty-seven member states, and to open new democratic opportunities within the European executive bloc itself. It is now up to political parties and civil society organizations to seize this opportunity to liberate European politics from the technocratic trenches and remove us from this pernicious alternative of helpless national retreat and the status quo of Brussels' economic policies.

—Translated by Paul Dermine

PART ONE

ANOTHER EUROPE
IS POSSIBLE

1

The Euro-ization of Europe

The Extra-mural Rise of a Government of the Euro and the Redefinition of the 'European Project'

GUILLAUME SACRISTE AND ANTOINE VAUCHEZ

As the economic and financial crisis has amply demonstrated, the euro now used by more than 350 million Europeans is much more than a single currency. For those who hope to defend it and ensure its stability, it has become the focal point for a widening range of government measures over the last two decades. The general view is that twenty-five years of economic and monetary unification under the aegis of the euro have made Europe unrecognizable in a number of respects. The Europe of the Single Market, centered on freedom of movement, has now been overshadowed by the powerful system of monitoring and disciplining of member-state economic policies "in the name of the euro," and the effects of this are now being felt at the heart of national social pacts. And the passionate debates of the early 2000s on the European political Constitution have given way to rather technical discussions about the "sub-optimality" of the euro and reform of how it is managed.

Although Europe has been changing significantly, the direction of the changes is not immediately visible to the naked eye. Lacking the clarity of classical constitutional architectures, the governance of the euro forces anyone really interested in it to try to fit together what first appear in scattered form like pieces of a jigsaw puzzle. Yet the investigation does reveal a long-term, though still incomplete and contested, process of the euro-ization of Europe. Three dimensions, in many respects inseparable from one another, define the terms of this process: (1) the emergence at the heart of the European Union of a powerful financial pole comprising treasury departments and central banks; (2) the consolidation of a European system of monitoring and control over the policies of member states, designed to ensure the medium- to long-term stability of the euro; and (3) the gradual construction of a new hierarchy in the European project, around the issues of financial stability, budgetary equilibrium, and structural reforms, which in the process marginalizes or subordinates the other poles of European policy (social Europe, basic rights, the environment).

In fact, the euro-ization of Europe is first and foremost a history of the rising power of a financial pole at the heart of the European project. This pole does not impose itself "from above" through a "Brussels dictate," nor "from outside"—which is not to say that it does not constitute a "supranational" elite. More precisely, it is an increasingly dense *transnational* network of financial bureaucracies and French, German, Italian, and other "treasury people," but also senior officials of the European Commission's DG ECFIN (Directorate-General for Economic and Financial Affairs) and national and European central bankers—a network that has taken shape with the adoption of the euro as the single currency. Trapped within the ever tighter social circle of EU preparatory committees and negotiations, these financial players have gradually mapped out a common agenda under the banner of budgetary consolidation and structural reforms. In establishing themselves over time as key to the credibility of member-states *and* of the euro vis-à-vis market players, they have acquired an ever stronger political capacity at the heart of the European project.

The phenomenon has found *institutional* expression in a new "extra-mural" European governance: that is, the governance of the euro, which for many lies outside the institutional framework of the European Union. The clearest token of this externality is the Eurogroup, the central nucleus of the system, which is renowned for its pivotal role in the crisis and has developed at a considerable distance from the democratic political control of national and European parliaments. Today, a whole multilateral system of monitoring (and disciplining) hems in governments in their definition of economic, budgetary, fiscal, and social policies. This system—which combines incentives and penalties, "soft law" and "hard law," recommendations with no effect, and memorandums listing in absurd detail the measures that member states should take forthwith to comply with financial assistance programs—has progressively sunk deeper roots into national policy-making.

It would be wrong to see this governance of the euro as just one more European public policy. By virtue of its growing importance, as well as the imbalances revealed by the crisis, it tends to become the *basic framework* for all other public policies, setting their preconditions or converting them into an "overriding obligation" of financial stability and budgetary balance. In this sense, euro-ization also designates the production of a new hierarchy within the European project, which operates in tandem with the oversight acquired by the technocratic financial pole. It is then easy to understand who are the real losers from this process today. Not so much member states per se, as is too often purported, but instead specific segments with them: the "welfare elites" in Berlin, Brussels, Paris, or Rome who champion the (relative) autonomy of policies bound up with the social state, and the players in the arena of representative politics (parties, national and European parliaments, or even ministers, who are often overshadowed by the autonomy progressively acquired by this transnational network of "financiers"), whose legitimacy to impel, co-ordinate, or steer the European project is considerably weakened.

The history in question here is therefore less the (economic) history of the eurozone than the history of its *governance:* that is to say, of the elites who sustain it, the policies that are formed by it, and the constraining effects that it produces. In this regard, the economic and financial crisis that broke out in 2008 is certainly a critical moment, but it features less as a point of departure or an original reason than as an accelerator or a coalescing factor for sets of solutions or measures defined since the late 1980s.

I. From the Delors Committee to the Eurogroup: A Demand for Independence

The re-tabling of the monetary union project on the EU agenda in the mid-1980s was the occasion for the emergence of a new group of players at the front of the European stage. This group, previously confined to secondary roles in the integration process, consisted of financial bureaucracies and central banks in the various member states but also at the EU level; it would play a key role in defining the institutions and policies of the governance of the euro. Coming as they did from "rival" institutions, these "financiers" caught up in the monetarist turn of the 1980s also found themselves "roped in" when it came to convincing their governments to construct the Economic and Monetary Union (EMU) safely away from the usual political and diplomatic arenas, under the control of an ad hoc structure of governance where the national and EU financial bureaucracies would run the show.

1. The Europe of Treasuries and Central Banks

At the beginning, the Monetary Committee—from which the powerful Eurogroup Working Group (EWG) directly descends—served as the preparatory committee for the Eurogroup. Created in 1957 under the Treaty of Rome, this first European monetary cadre was only supposed to promote the *coordination* of member states in monetary matters, to the extent that this was necessary for the functioning of the Common Market. The member states nominated two members each, "known for their competence in the monetary domain," one from the finance ministry (generally, the head of the Treasury) and the other from the central bank (generally, its deputy governor). The European Commission, which provided the secretariat of the Committee, was also represented on it by the director-general of the DG ECFIN and the director of monetary affairs. When it became clear in 1964 that central bank governors needed to be more closely associated in order to coordinate these European monetary policies, a second committee, the Committee of Governors of the Central Banks, was constituted. The two committees, endowed with exclusive competence in monetary matters, were mainly occupied in managing the "European currency snake," a mechanism established in 1972 that was supposed to make it possible to limit exchange-rate fluctuations among countries belonging to the European Communities.

Early "club effects" began to develop inside them, however; the secretary of the Monetary Committee, in his report on its workings, did not hesitate to describe it as a "fraternity." Without even speaking of the often similar backgrounds and concerns of members of this Committee, it should be said that its statutes had been conceived in such a way as to encourage the development of horizontal links over and above national affiliations. They stipulated, for example, that its members were appointed on a personal basis and exercised their functions in complete independence, in the general interests of the Community. Committee meetings were also marked by confidentiality, so that its members should feel free to divulge certain information or to reveal any reservations they might have. Initially it published brief annual reports on its activities, but these were stopped in 1988 by tacit and mutual consent, turning the Committee into one of the rare European institutions whose functioning became less and less transparent as it gained in power.[1]

Shortly after his arrival in Brussels, in January 1985, the new president of the Commission, Jacques Delors, experienced the strength of this first group of European monetary leaders. He tried to enlarge the competence of the Commission on monetary issues within the framework of negotiations for the Single European Act—the new European treaty eventually signed in 1986 that was supposed to relaunch the European integration agenda by establishing a "single market"—with an appeal to the highest political authorities, F. Mitterrand and H. Kohl. However, the group of representatives of financial bureaucracies, with the Bundesbank president at its head, imposed its own preserve: monetary questions, it insisted, could not become a European Community's competence, placed, like everything touching on the construction of the Single Market, under the control of the Commission. Because it affected the sovereignty of member states (and the reserved domain of treasury departments and central banks), the Monetary Committee also claimed a central role in the event of further developments toward Monetary Union, as the text of the Single Act ultimately envisaged.

This initial setback led Delors to think that, if it was to get its way within this group of financial bureaucrats, the Commission—without a currency or a sovereign state to defend—should blend in with the group! So, in contrast to his predecessors, Delors made a point, early in his mandate, of participating in the monthly meetings of the Committee of Governors of the Central Banks at the headquarters of the Bank of International Settlements in Basel—even if it meant suffering the humiliation of not being invited to all the official dinners organized by the governors at the prestigious hotels in the city! He gathered around him a team of monetary specialists who in their profile, and their pan-European proclivities, strongly resembled the members of the two committees in charge of European monetary affairs. Thus, Jean-Paul Mingasson, a senior French official from the Treasury, headed the monetary leadership of the Commission's DG ECFIN (a body *directly* attached to the presidency), while Tommaso Padoa-Schioppa, one of the directors of the Banca d'Italia who had himself been director of the DG ECFIN, served as special adviser to President Delors on monetary matters. Also, the group of economists who worked with Padoa-Schioppa in 1986 to define the Commission's new monetary doctrine (report: "Efficiency, Stability and Equity") included the future governor of the Bank of Greece and future vice president of the ECB, Lucas Papademos; the future governor of the Bank of England, Mervyn King; and the director of forecasting in the French finance ministry, Jean-Claude Milleron.

This "entrist" strategy of the Commission in relation to the circles in which European monetary policy was debated came to a head at the Hannover Summit in 1988 with the constitution of the famous "Delors Committee," a think tank that has gone down in history as having laid the theoretical and institutional groundwork for the Economic and Monetary Union (EMU).[2] Although, at Delors's own request, central bankers were preeminent in the Committee, this time he chaired the committee and chose its key members (notably including one of its rapporteurs, the inevitable Tommaso Padoa-Schioppa). So it was that Delors managed to establish legitimacy within the group of financiers and central bankers who "managed" the deepening of the Economic and Monetary Union.

Although heterogeneous in terms of the institutional interests it defended (national treasuries, central banks, the European Commission), the network that developed in this way was very coherent at a theoretical level. It should be said that since the 1980s, under the influence of monetarist theory and the challenge to Keynesian schemas, a set of pivotal arenas straddling the world of monetary policy and the world of academia had prepared the ground by sketching the principles of a new monetary policy. In the early 1980s, for example, at a series of seminars organized by the economist Robert Triffin, a part of the community of central bankers, together with senior officials in the European Commission and a number of academics, had put forward a common basis for the relaunch of European monetary union. One of the most important ideas to emerge from these discussions was a consensus that, in a context of complete liberalization of capital, the main objective of any reform of European monetary policy had to be the struggle against inflation.[3] This emphasis on price stability was itself the result of a sea change in economic theory at the time, beginning with a reinterpretation of the famous Philips curve to the effect that the rate of inflation cannot be manipulated (at least in the long term) in order to boost job creation; such an objective could be achieved only through the establishment of an independent central bank, which alone could guarantee the "credibility" of a common monetary policy. According to the formula advanced by the economists Francesco Giavazzi and Marco Pagano in 1988, "the advantage of tying one's hands"[4] by handing over monetary policy to an independent institution lay in the greater monetary "credibility" it afforded.

2. Institutional Separatism

In short, the single currency presupposed a set of *specific* institutions, alone capable of creating the zone of economic and financial *stability* necessary for it to function well. An independent central bank was, to be sure, the foundation for the whole EMU. But more broadly this also required centers of consultation and decision, such as the Eurogroup, that would be sheltered from the political arbitration of diplomats in the Committee of Permanent Representatives (COREPER, the key structure coordinating member-state administrations since the birth of the European Communities) and kept at a safe distance from national or European parliamentary controls. This type of mantra would inspire the emergent group of European "financiers," headed by the Monetary Committee, when the time came to define the institutions in charge of the euro. By creating a special autonomous stage for economic and monetary affairs, with specialist players from the financial bureaucracies and central banks, the way was opening to an "extramural" government of the euro.

The opening act of this institutional separatism was undoubtedly the *duplication* of negotiating arenas in the run-up to the Maastricht Treaty, involving *two* distinct intergovernmental conferences (IGCs), so that the players and issues of the "Political Union" IGC were split off from those of the "Economic and Monetary Union" IGC. The secretary of state in the German finance ministry, Horst Köhler, a member of the Monetary

Committee from 1990 to 1993 and the future president of the Federal Republic, played a decisive role in this decision. In his view, as well as that of the minister under whom he served, Theo Waigel, the purpose of the duplication was to free economic and monetary issues from political interference. In fact, the EMU IGC negotiators initially came from the "fraternity" of members of the Monetary Committee: Horst Köhler for the Germans, Jean-Claude Trichet for the French, Nigel Wicks for the British, Cees Maas for the Dutch, Mario Sarcinelli and then Mario Draghi for the Italians, Yves Mersch for Luxembourg, and so on. All were former—and future—core players of the emerging transnational pole of "financiers."

The policy of *institutional duplication* did not end there; its main crystallization point came in 1997 with the creation of the Eurogroup, an unofficial structure that periodically brings together euro-area finance ministers, the European Commissioner for Economic and Financial Affairs, and a member of the ECB directorate (which was set up soon after the creation of the Eurogroup). The creation of this "economic government" of the euro, supported by Lionel Jospin's Socialist government in France, initially encountered widespread opposition: Tony Blair fiercely rejected any such autonomous institutional pole outside of EU institutions; the Germans feared a return to French-style *dirigisme;* and the young ECB was mainly concerned to assert its own independence and external position in relation to European policy. Thus, the body (called first Euro X, then Eurogroup) that had been created "to discuss questions linked to the special responsibilities they share vis-à-vis the single currency"[5] was actually such a body only on condition that it met informally, exchanged views in confidence, and remained completely *outside* the institutional framework of the European Community. These were all reasons that made it successful as the main locus for political-administrative coordination of the eurozone. Beyond having a role in the exchange of information and assessments concerning the economic situation—which is proving very useful for the smallest countries in the eurozone, which lack the means to develop their own economic expertise—the Eurogroup structures have become the main site where interpretive frameworks and practical conditions are established for implementation of the many coordinating instruments and objectives that the government of the euro has adopted over time, beginning with the Stability and Growth Pact (1997) and the European Semester (2010).

Usually meeting on the eve of official sessions of the Economic and Financial Affairs Council (ECOFIN), the Eurogroup has preempted ECOFIN's decisions, as the euro-area issues were progressively taking up most of Europe's economic agenda. One example is the nomination of members of the ECB directorate, where the Eurogroup has behaved as a powerful caucus and ECOFIN has been content to ratify decisions made and discussed elsewhere. The Growth and Stability Pact of 2005 was also amended within the Eurogroup before the decision was ratified by ECOFIN. And it was in the Eurogroup that opposition was mounted to Sarkozy's proposed unilateral suspension of VAT on oil products in response to soaring prices, and so on. As one of the most knowledge-able analysts in this sphere, Jean Pisani-Ferry, pointed out as early as 2006, the Eurogroup has gradually changed "from a mere talking shop into what increasingly looks like a policy-making institution." Indeed, a new institutional duplication soon appeared to be necessary—hence the creation in 2004 of a *specific* preparatory committee for the Eurogroup, the Eurogroup Working Group (EWG), in parallel to the Economic and Financial Committee (ECF) in charge of preparing ECOFIN, a structure that quickly imposed itself as the mainspring of this new governmental structure. With a touch of irony, the Lisbon Treaty of 2007 assisted in the consolidation of this "extramural" government by formally recog-nizing the "informal" character of Eurogroup meetings and by ac-knowledging the "specific responsibilities" that the member states shared by virtue of the single currency.

3. An "Extramural" Government

In response to the sovereign debt crisis that broke out in April 2010, with the announcement of the risk of a Greek default, the parallel Eurogroup structure quickly asserted itself as the main arena for management of the crisis. The clearest evidence for this is the unprecedented duplica-tion of meetings at every level of this structure for governance of the euro. With no fewer than 206 meetings between 2010 and 2017 (an av-erage of one every two weeks), the Eurogroup of finance ministers con-stituted the main political organism where responses to the crisis were thrashed out—assisted at the gravest moments by a new governing stratum created in 2008, the Euro Summits, consisting of heads of state and government together with the presidents of the Commission and

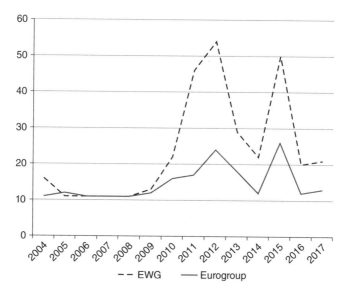

Number of Meetings per Year (2004-2017) Eurogroup and
Eurogroup Working Group (based on Eurogroup data)

(*Eurogroup:* Eurozone finance ministers, European Commissioner for
Economic and Financial Affairs, and a member of the ECB Directorate.
EWG (Eurogroup Working Group): Two senior officials from the
finance ministry of each eurozone country, the director of the DG
ECFIN, and two senior executives of the ECB.)

the ECB. But it was the EWG—consisting of top officials from finance
ministries, the ECB, and the Commission—that operated as the main
hub of this new European directorate. It met 264 times during the same
eight-year period (2010–2017)—that is, no fewer than 33 times a year.

Along the way, the transnational network of "financiers" consolidated. The reservations that the first ECB president, Wim Duisenberg,
had initially expressed to the Eurogroup in 2001 concerning that network's participation ("The euro-area monetary and fiscal authorities
cannot and will not coordinate our respective policy areas ex ante")[6]
rapidly faded away. Now the ECB was participating in Eurogroup meetings at every political and administrative level, directly associated with
the definition of memorandums of understanding (MoUs) but also
with their implementation through its involvement in the Troika (IMF,
European Commission, ECB). Raised to the role of chief regulator of
the European banking sector with the creation of the Single Supervi-

sory Mechanism of European banks, the ECB would be directly involved in political reflection about the future of the eurozone within
the framework of the Group of Four Presidents (the presidents of the
ECB, Commission, Eurogroup, European Council—a circle from which
the president of the European Parliament would initially be excluded).
All these stages indicate an ever closer union of the national and European financial bureaucracies.

Thus, situated at the geometrical point where all the players in the
government of the euro intersect, the Eurogroup has considerably expanded its sphere of influence in the framework of the crisis, adding to
the decisions it takes affecting the core economic, fiscal, and social policies of member states. One thinks, for instance, of the decision taken in
the middle of the night, March 15–16, 2013, to levy a tax of 6.75% on
all Cypriot bank accounts below 100,000 euros—a compromise that
none of the participants would take responsibility for the next morning!
But above all one thinks of the marathon negotiations over the memorandums of understanding and the lists of economic, fiscal, budgetary,
and social reforms tied to the granting of financial assistance to Greece—
in response to which Pierre Moscovici (a man who knows the Eurogroup
inside out, having regularly attended its meetings as French finance
minister in 2012–2014 and as Commissioner for Economic and Financial Affairs ever since) remarked: "We are deciding behind closed doors
the fate of 11 million people." In the context of the crisis, the Eurogroup
imposed itself as the chief political and administrative supervisor of
states placed "under program" (Cyprus, Greece, Ireland, Portugal, Spain),
ensuring strict observance of the budget shock and fiscal strategy ad-
ministered in the framework of the memorandum in question, but also
of the "post-program" procedure that maintains a tight control over national policy choices in these member states. However, the expanded
governmental role of the Eurogroup can also be seen in the "structural
reforms" agenda that developed in the mid-2010s. Basing itself on the
DG ECFIN's "Analytical Notes," the Eurogroup has now taken up the
responsibility to review a wide range of fiscal, social, and educational
matters—labor tax law, investment, pension stability, insolvency framework, spending reviews, human capital (education policy), and so
on—from its particular angle of financial stability and budgetary consolidation. These are all issues about which the European financial
bureaucracies now agree on a common viewpoint ("best practices,"

"benchmarks," "recommendations"), which they undertake to defend upon their return to their respective capitals.

This institution *sui generis*, born on the fringe of the treaties, has become pivotal to the governance of the euro yet continues to elude the common rules of transparency and responsibility associated with political institutions. Probably it was the appointment of the media-savvy Yanis Varoufakis as Greek finance minister, at the very height of the crisis, that really brought into the open its habits of confidentiality and secrecy. As Jan-Werner Müller indicates, certain "veterans of European integration like the German finance minister Wolfgang Schäuble saw him as a vandal in the engine-room of the EU, where the expectation is that dirty deals can be made comfortably and in secret."[7] Rather late in the day, the EU ombudsman expressed alarm at this complete opacity, pointing to the "economic, financial and societal impact of the decisions taken by [the Eurogroup]." Even though the Eurogroup president consented to publish draft agendas of the Eurogroup and very general summaries of the discussions (rather than the actual proceedings or detailed minutes of the various positions), he did not agree to touch the core issue, the "range of bodies and services [that] prepare Eurogroup meetings" and form the quasi-permanent structure of euro-area government.[8]

In short, the crisis will have further entrenched the institutional separatism of the government of the euro. The adoption of two ad hoc international treaties—treaties that are external to the European Union, and therefore to mechanisms of political control inherent in the single institutional framework of the EU—will complete the edifice. One of these, the Treaty on Stability, Coordination and Governance (otherwise known as the Fiscal Compact), signed in March 2012, completed the *external* institutionalization of the government of the euro, by enshrining a political level with the Euro Summits of nineteen heads of state and government and (quite secondary) the ad hoc interparliamentary committee confined to a purely consultative role. The other treaty, establishing the European Stability Mechanism (ESM), in 2012 replaced a European stabilization fund created as a matter of urgency by the member states. Based on treaty-defined pro rata contributions and voting rights of member states, the ESM constitutes a financial lever capable of mobilizing up to 700 billion euros to provide assistance *with conditions* to member states in difficulty. With a composition identical to that of the Eurogroup, it is placed under the tutelage of the Eurogroup president, who decides on the granting of financial assistance, the payment of various tranches, and the follow-on "policy of conditionality" imposed on the state that is "under program."

Thus, from the ECB to the Eurogroup, from the EWG to the Euro Summits, also taking in the Troika and the European Stability Mechanism, a whole "extramural" political-administrative space has been consolidated for the governance of the euro. In this half-intergovernmental, half-supranational hybrid framework, constructed at a good distance from political and parliamentary controls, a powerful system has been able to develop for the surveillance of member-state policies under the threefold sign of financial stability, budgetary consolidation, and structural reforms.

II. A Gouvernment of National Social and Economic Pacts

In short, the euro was supposed to be "governed" (in the French version) or at least "framed" (in the German version). But few players in the financial pole believed so fervently in the virtues of the market as to think it capable, through its own powers of coordination alone, of ensuring the convergence of economic and budgetary performance among eurozone countries. From the first negotiations on the euro, the "financiers" (headed by the Monetary Committee) defined the framework: that is, the creation of the economic and financial *zone of stability* necessary for the medium- to long-term viability of the single currency presupposed a system of multilateral surveillance, with a subtle mix of constraints and incentives that would both bind and orient national economic policies.[9] In practice, the aim was to place the policies and performance of member states under the surveillance of ECOFIN, the European Commission, and other member states' treasuries.

In terms of policy orientation, this new economic convergence machinery marked a clear break with the early European texts on economic policy convergence going back to 1974, which had been based on Keynesian considerations in their quest for "stability, growth and full employment."[10] From the first text adopted in 1990, multilateral surveillance was firmly geared to supply-side policies, the main economic policy of member states no longer being full employment but "sustained non-inflationary growth" centered on price stability, "sound" public finances, "healthy" monetary conditions, and an "open competitive market."

1. Disciplining National Economic Policies

This basic framework for multilateral surveillance, and its grip on the economic and budgetary policies of eurozone countries, would constantly tighten. In the course of reforms, the areas covered by multilateral surveillance grew in number; the information that member states were asked to supply in "response" to ECOFIN's "recommendations" and "formal notices" became more and more precise and comprehensive; timetables became tighter and forced member states into hasty responses; and the penalty procedures against backsliding states were strengthened and streamlined.

It is also necessary to differentiate between the two pillars on which this multilateral machinery of surveillance was constructed: one relating to the control of national budgetary policies, the other to the coordination of their economic policies. Right from the start, budgetary policy was thought of as clearly distinct from other economic policies, and as justifying much more binding injunctions. In this domain, the Maastricht Treaty had envisaged numerically quantified targets (the famous "Maastricht convergence criteria," which designated upper thresholds of 3% of GDP for the government deficit and 60% for the national debt) and allowed for clearly defined pecuniary penalties. An "Excessive Deficit Procedure" (EDP) was established, with the aim of compelling governments to respect these reference values. In 1997—in the highly sensitive period of transition to the euro, when the German political and financial elites were worried about the risks that EMU entailed for the German "culture of stability"—the Excessive Deficit Procedure acquired a more direct mandatory character. The adoption of a "Stability Pact" fixed a timetable that bound governments to give a continuous account of their budgetary efforts and to correct any deviations from the budgetary norm, on pain of a fine consisting of a fixed component equal to 0.2% of the previous year's GDP and a variable component of up to 0.5% of the country's GDP.

The second pillar—coordination of economic policies—was conceived in a different way, as incentivizing and nonbinding. Because it had implications for key areas of national social pacts (economic policies, welfare state, labor market, and so on), this pillar at first involved mechanisms of incentivization and cooperation consisting of recommendations, peer reviews, benchmarking, and, if necessary, blaming. ECOFIN's definition of Broad Economic Policy Guidelines (BEPGs), relating to economic and budgetary policies, structural reforms, wage bargaining, and such, was supposed to permit the insertion of governments into a process of convergence. In this, the Commission had the role of prosecutor—monitoring, and informing ECOFIN about, an ever larger battery of indicators; individual governments had the role of defense counsel, responding to recommendations and backing this up with corrective programs; and ECOFIN had the role of judge, stepping in and deciding in the last instance with regard to recommendations and penalties. A government that did not comply with these broad guidelines might, if the Commission proposed it, be issued with public recommendations by ECOFIN, whose public character was considered sufficient to trigger the verdict of the financial markets and rating agencies. Over time, just like for the Excessive Deficit Procedure, the BEPGs would become increasingly intrusive: at first, they gave only an extremely vague and general set of indications that mainly reiterated the objectives of the Maastricht Treaty (price stability, sound public finances, job creation, reduction of indirect labor costs, and so on), but they gradually expanded to all areas of economic and social policy, becoming more and more precise along the way. In December 1993, three guidelines had been developed over four pages without any specific recommendations to member states; ten years later, 23 guidelines and 94 country-specific recommendations were issued for the 2003–2005 period alone.[11]

The sovereign debt crisis, understood as the result of the weakness of this system of multilateral surveillance, was an opportunity to toughen the control machinery—by strengthening the role of the prosecutor—the European Commission and the system's coercive bite over member states. In December 2011, a deep reform was introduced through a package of directives, the so-called Six-Pack and Two-Pack, which considerably reinforced the pillars of surveillance and placed them under the single umbrella of the so-called European Semester, an integrative framework bringing together both economic and budgetary instruments of policy coordination and surveillance. This reinforced the surveillance of economic policies, extending it to fiscal and social policies, and hardened it through the creation of a Macroeconomic Imbalance Procedure

(MIP) modeled on the Excessive Deficit Procedure. Emblematically, the ten economic, financial, and structural indicators of its "scoreboard"—from the "current account balance" to the "nominal unit labor cost," taking in the "general government sector debt," the "evolution of property prices," and so forth—were supposed to allow the early detection of "macroeconomic imbalances." The budgetary pillar, the Excessive Deficit Procedure, was also reinforced, because the recommendations of the Commission in terms of penalties (for a country under the Excessive Deficit Procedure that did not comply with formal notices) were now considered to have been adopted "unless a qualified majority of states *opposed* them" within ECOFIN (a "reverse majority vote" that would be much more difficult for the defiant state to achieve).

Another novelty of the "European Semester" (see Table 1) was that it integrated and synchronized the two pillars in the same timing, which now followed the *budgetary* timetable of member states in such a way as to maximize impact on the choice of economic and social orientations. The *European* Semester, centered on evaluating the performance of the economic and budgetary policies of the member states, is now supposed to precede the "national" Semester during the last six months of the year, which corresponds to the time given to member states to implement the guidelines or recommendations so defined.

2. The Co-Ruling of Countries "under Memorandum"

European surveillance in general has become much stricter, but it has developed an altogether more heavy-handed quality in the case of member states that are receiving European financial assistance (Cyprus, Greece, Ireland, Portugal, Spain). When on April 23, 2010, a few months after revealing that its national debt had been grossly underestimated, the Greek government issued an appeal for European financial aid, the EU established a special contingency fund. A first sum of 80 billion euros was already released on May 2, 2010. Based on inspiration directly from the IMF, however, the aid was granted only in exchange for strict and highly demanding commitments by the state "under program." Two new funding plans were signed in March 2012 and July 2015, each accompanied with an "Economic Adjustment Program." The memorandums of understanding included drastic austerity measures (government budget cuts, increased flexibility of the labor market, massive privatiza-

Table 1   The Annual Calendar for the 'European Semester' (since 2011)

October	Member states in the eurozone submit their draft budgets; the Commission assesses them in terms of the obligations of the Stability Pact. It issues notices in relation to countries covered by an Excessive Deficit Procedure.
November	The European Commission presents the *Annual Growth Survey* (AGS), which sets the EU's economic, social, and fiscal priorities for the coming year, and an *Alert Mechanism Report* (AMR) identifying member states that, in respect of a "scoreboard" of socioeconomic indicators defined under the Macroeconomic Imbalance Procedure, are susceptible to further assessment in an *In-Depth Review* (IDR).
March	On this basis, the Commission produces *Country-Specific Reports* (CSRs) on macroeconomic imbalances in member states, which it may accompany with recommendations.
April	Taking the CSRs into account, member states present their National Reform Programs listing the "structural reforms" they have in view. They also present their Stability Program, which should set out medium-term budgetary objectives within the framework of the Stability and Growth Pact.
May	Once it has examined the Action Programs of the member states, the Commission produces Country-Specific Recommendations (CSRs), particularly for the opening (or closing) of an Excessive Deficit Procedure, which are then examined and adopted by ECOFIN and the European Council.

tion, deep reforms of the social protection, pensions, and health systems and of education and public administration). Because these do not include inscribed guarantees of minimum protection in terms of social and economic rights, they will directly affect the social balance of member states. Their recessionary consequences and serious social impact have been widely highlighted by a number of NGOs and by various international bodies (such as the International Labor Organization, and the European Committee of Social Rights—Council of Europe). During the crisis years, the Eurogroup decided on and operated similar (though less massive) programs in Ireland (December 2010), Portugal (June 2011),

Extract from the Third Memorandum of Understanding between the European Commission acting on behalf of the European Stability Mechanism and the Hellenic Republic and the Bank of Greece, August 19, 2015

- *"Restoring fiscal sustainability:* Greece will target a medium-term primary surplus of 3.5% of GDP to be achieved through a combination of upfront parametric fiscal reforms, including to its VAT and pension system, supported by an ambitious programme to strengthen tax compliance and public financial management, and fight tax evasion, while ensuring adequate protection of vulnerable groups.

- *Safeguarding financial stability:* Greece will immediately take steps to tackle Non-Performing Loans (NPLs). A recapitalization process of banks should be completed before the end of 2015, which will be accompanied by concomitant measures to strengthen the governance of the Hellenic Financial Stability Fund (HFSF) and of banks.

- *Growth, competitiveness and investment:* Greece will design and implement a wide range of reforms in labour markets and product markets (including energy) that not only ensure full compliance with EU requirements, but which also aim at achieving European best practices. There will be an ambitious privatization programme, and policies which support investment.

- A modern State and public administration shall be a key priority of the programme. Particular attention will be paid to increasing the efficiency of the public sector in the delivery of essential public goods and services. Measures will be taken to enhance the efficiency of the judicial system and to upgrade the fight against corruption. Reforms will strengthen the institutional and operational independence of key institutions such as revenue administration and the statistics institute (ELSTAT)."

Spain (July 2012), and Cyprus (March 2013). Although these countries have since exited from the Economic Adjustment Programs, they remain under Eurogroup surveillance in the framework of "post-program monitoring," which involves biannual inspections followed by reports and the possibility of new corrective measures.

III. *The Re-Ordering of the European Project*

Assessing the binding and coercive power of this emerging eurozone government is not an easy task. Except for countries "under memorandum," where it is implacable, it does not primarily lie where it is customarily found—namely, in the power to impose penalties. To take only the example of the Excessive Deficit Procedure, none of the forty "procedures" initiated by the Commission over the years has yet resulted in a duly formalized penalty. In reality, the penalties do not have the automatic character sometimes attributed to them, both because the procedure involves many veto-players capable of blocking or slowing down the penalization, and because context-specific and country-specific considerations come into play at each stage of this complex process. The Commission itself has been keen to show that the European Semester is "based on guidance, not on corrections," pointing at the room available for political margins of maneuvering. This is most clearly seen in the Commission's decision to take (or not to take) action after a country has passed one of the "alert thresholds" built into the "scoreboard"; or in the way in which the Commission takes account of a member state's political and economic context in drafting its recommendations; or in its decision to follow through (or not) on the penalty procedure for excessive deficits, as in July 2016 when Portugal escaped *in extremis* the penalties for which it seemed to have been marked down.

Besides, it is often very difficult to identify a "decision-maker" in this multiheaded game. The procedures of the "European Semester" consist of a series of microdecisions involving multiple committees and institutions, so that the policy outcome *gradually* solidifies through successive sedimentations and consensuses. It is therefore necessary to give up trying to identify *one* person or institution responsible for a decision, or *one* level that wins out over the others. It is not "Europe," or even "the Commission," that imposes itself "from outside" on national governments, any more than it is one country (even Germany) that alone imposes its choices in the complex procedural framework of the "European Semester." The binding power in the government of the euro is more complex: it derives from a more diffuse, though no less powerful, process involving the development of a new hierarchy in the European project, which has gradually positioned the group of "financiers" (and the issues they prioritize) as the primary definers of European public policies (and of the conditions of their legitimacy).

The main point here is that the network of European financial bureaucracies has all the time been growing in consistency. Of course, many things separate these senior treasury and central bank officials from one another: the state or institution they represent, their belonging to the group of "creditor" or "debtor" countries, and so on. But they are now caught up in a powerful dynamic of integration. The intense sociability of the crisis years, which clogged up the diaries of senior officials in the financial pole, is undoubtedly one factor, as is the (relative) closeness of the places where they trained and of their theoretical positions. Also important is the length of time they have spent in the network: whether they have remained in certain key positions without a break, as in the case of Marco Buti (who has been director-general of the DG ECFIN since 2008, after two further years as deputy director-general), or whether they have circulated between the different (national and European) poles of this governance of the euro, like the current president of the EWG (since 2017), Hans Vijbrief, who from 2012 to 2017 was treasury director in the Netherlands, accompanying his minister (for a time, Jeroen Djisselboem) to every meeting of the Eurogroup, but was also chairman of the board of directors of the European Financial Stability Facility, the ancestor of today's ESM. The coming together of this transnational network of "financiers" is all the stronger because meetings of senior Eurogroup or ESM officials have never been seen as political and diplomatic arenas, but rather as technical forums subject to the constraints of "problem-solving" and efficiency.[12] Everything—from the confidentiality of discussions, which the Eurogroup president defends tooth and nail, to the choice of decision making by consensus over voting (thereby weakening the capacity to express dissenting opinions)—indicates that Eurogroup or ESM meetings aim primarily to produce a common viewpoint or crisis solutions. In short, this powerful endogenous dynamic favors mutual apprenticeship mechanisms, by inducing each member to take his partners' political constraints into account, but also the formation of shared norms (concerning the credibility of eurozone governments and institutions or the range of economic policy solutions considered practicable).

This transnational financial pole has acquired an essential brokering position as the political interface between European institutions and national governments. In effect, it is a directorate partly autonomous of national and EU political-administrative spaces, but also partly embedded on a lasting basis in those spaces. No doubt this is the reason for its special power and capacity to frame the course of economic and monetary policies in Europe. Those involved in it know that once decisions have been taken or forms of agreement worked out, there is a good chance that they will also be approved in the political-administrative machinery of the member states. At least every member can count on the fact that the other participants will try to get their governments and civil services to endorse them, by mobilizing the authority they possess in their national political-administrative domain. The political imprint of this bureaucratic network in the definition of European policy priorities stems precisely from its intermediate position at the heart of both EU *and* national policy-making. In other words, the political authority acquired by this new transnational governing elite cannot be simply equated with the formal coercive power it acquired during the crisis. It lies in the more profound, yet less visible, transformation of the European project.

1. The (New) Conditions for States' Political Credibility

The binding effects of this governance of the euro have made themselves felt in the changes it has conferred on European politics itself. Two decades of EMU have profoundly transformed the ways in which the credibility of member states is gauged. It is not possible here to trace all the stages in this process, which has made respect for the "Maastricht criteria" the condition for the overall legitimacy and political weight of a member state in European affairs. The obligation to anchor the golden budgetary rule (a balanced budget) in the member states' constitutions— which was imposed in 2012 under the Fiscal Compact—symbolized this new order in the core of the member states. Emmanuel Macron's position that the French government would not have the legitimacy to regain the political initiative in the EU unless it had first "done its duty" (that is, left the "Excessive Deficit Procedure" it had entered in 2009) confirmed this from a different angle. European political authority is thus partly dependent on a country's position on the "debtor-creditor" scale of values, thereby transmitting to the European project forms of valuation characteristic of rating agencies or players in the government securities market.

Another way of seeing this shift is in terms of incorporation into the heart of public administration, through the general reorganization that national or EU administrations have progressively initiated to maintain their standing and their credibility in this new European government.

Thus, the Commission has thoroughly redrawn its organization charts and its policy instruments as its role as chief prosecutor in the monitoring of member states has asserted itself. It has done this in such a way as to be capable of generating the expertise and forecasting necessary to produce the multiple reports by country and sector (employment, labor market, pensions system, and so on) that are part of its remit within the system of multilateral surveillance. Lacking the direct coercive power to get its notices and recommendations respected, the Commission has based its power instead on its capacity for expert and quantitative assessment of the economic state of the euro area. Eurostat, the Commission's statistical bureau, has played a new role here. Since 1995 it has been collecting data on national debts and excessive deficits (to which a number of other areas will soon be added), and the Commission uses these as the basis for its notices and recommendations to member states.[13] With the creation of a special directorate (B4) for economic statistics and economic and monetary convergence, the Commission added to the existing expertise of the DG ECFIN a capacity for measuring and comparing the public deficits and debts of candidates for membership of the single currency—a capacity that would soon prove politically decisive. It is true that Eurostat must still base itself on data provided by national authorities, but the adoption in 2010 of the European System of Accounts (ESA) as the common standard for economic and budgetary data means that it has become the indispensable player. Indeed, after the Greek statistical fiasco came to light in 2009, precipitating the European financial crisis, ECOFIN gave Eurostat the powers to audit national statistics.

But the DG ECFIN is unquestionably the administrative structure that has been strengthened the most. In charge of drafting and monitoring budgetary rules, it produces the Broad Economic Policy Guidelines (BEPGs), which involve economic and budgetary forecasting, and drafts the alerts and recommendations issued to member states. In a climate of cost-cutting within the Commission, it has nevertheless been significantly strengthened through a sharp rise in its staff and the creation of new units capable of producing knowledge in the domain of other DGs (DG EMPL, DG TAXUD), especially with regard to the labor market, but always within an "ECFIN perspective." In this rearming of the EU administration, we should not forget the role of the Secretariat-General of the European Commission in coordinating the various DGs affected by the "European Semester" (DG EMPL, DG TAXUD, in addition to the DG ECFIN and Eurostat), but also in monitoring the Troika's implementation of the memorandums (Structural Reform Support Service).

National administrations, for their part, have followed a mirror-image evolution. Now on the defensive in relation to the multilateral surveillance procedures, they have also reorganized to prepare, negotiate, and discuss the various documents and programs produced throughout the "European Semester" (see Box 1). For lack of deeper investigation, it remains difficult to assess the extent to which the principal ministries, beginning with the finance ministry, have become the "cheese structures" evoked by Yanis Varoufakis with regard to the ministry he headed in the first Tsipras government: that is, structures partly "governed," or at least hemmed in, by this dense network of transnational coordination spearheaded by the Eurogroup.[14] Everything indicates, however, that the governance of the euro (and the European system of multilateral surveillance) has sunk deep roots into the administrative levels of member states. There can be no doubt that it is helping to consolidate the role of finance departments in defining the actual position of the government, most notably within the "European Semester." One of the surest effects of these processes is the considerable strengthening of the interministerial role of finance ministries in coordinating the European position of their respective national governments—thereby undermining the traditional position of foreign ministries and permanent representatives of member states in Brussels, whose role has been accordingly reduced. Or perhaps the effect is that the competence now expected for the role of permanent representative (ambassador) in Brussels presupposes monetary and financial expertise, which is unevenly distributed among diplomats!

2. Tutelage of Economic and Social Policies

It is true that this gradual shift of the center of gravity in European politics has not taken place without resistance or countermobilizations.

When the definition of the Europe's Broad Economic Policy Guidelines (BEPGs) was being firmly placed under the authority of the financial pole, with the main priorities being the struggle against inflation, budgetary equilibrium, and major financial balances, the mid-1990s saw a countermobilization of the European "social pole" encouraged by the coming to power of Social Democratic governments in a majority of EU-15 countries. In 1994 this attempted rebalancing took shape in Essen in the European Council's launching of a "European Employment Strategy" (EES). Later enshrined in the Amsterdam Treaty in 1997, it was supposed to promote the development of a skilled, well-trained, and adaptable workforce, as well as labor markets capable of reacting rapidly to the evolution of the economy. An Employment Committee, modeled on the Monetary Committee, had even been created in 1995 to enable senior officials in labor and employment ministries to coordinate their work on the EES and to counterbalance the increasing role of ECOFIN.

This Employment Committee was also supposed to help extend the range of the Broad Economic Policy Guidelines by including the key points in the European Employment Strategy. In reality, however, as the "Lisbon strategy" adopted by heads of state and government in March 2000 would confirm, the BEPGs ultimately remained the sole responsibility of ECOFIN—a fact underlined by their assigned task of establishing "the medium to long-term consequences of structural reform policies to tap the potential for economic growth, employment and social cohesion, as well as the transition to a knowledge economy."[15] In fact, at the Commission it was the DG ECFIN that gradually imposed its leadership in the definition and monitoring of the Lisbon strategy and the BEPGs. And significantly, in December 2005 it also developed the annual LABREF database on labor market reforms, which tracked the taxes on labor, the length of work time, labor legislation, and so on in all member states, as well as the LIME (Lisbon Methodology) assessment framework, which allowed it to compare progress in "structural reforms" by member states, as defined in 2000 in the "Lisbon Strategy." Thus, in the middle of the first decade of this century, the financial pole—ECOFIN, the Economic and Financial Committee, and the DG ECFIN—largely established their tutelage over the definition of the EU's economic and social policies.

In many respects the "European Semester" consolidates this process of "economization of the social," binding the social and environmental

pole, through "structural reforms," to the machinery of multilateral surveillance. If the DGs and groups linked to these poles have seen benefits in the "European Semester" as a powerful lever of influence over
the policies of member states—in so far as it "socializes" or "greens" the
scoreboard of macroeconomic indicators used for the assessment of economic policy convergence—this has happened only with the proviso
that they agree to play the role of junior partner. In fact, social rights
and safeguards or environmental factors are integrated only marginally, and anyway most often abstractly, placing a question mark over
the relative autonomy of these sectors that are now placed under the
"European Semester" umbrella.

3. The Marginalization of Parliaments

As to the representative politics of parties and parliaments, it has never
had a good press in the "financial" pole. According to a doctrine force-
fully asserted in the 1980s, their versatility (or "inconsistency over time")
constituted a real threat to the policy of budgetary and financial stability.
Their "credibility" was far from proven, especially if compared with what
independent authorities such as central banks were able to offer. In
fact, one result of the Maastricht Treaty negotiations that went almost
unnoticed was the ejection of national parliaments and the European
Parliament from the system of economic policy coordination of member
states. The European Parliament was confined to a purely consultative
role, with no say in the drafting of BEPGs or recommendations issued
by ECOFIN to member states. At the very most, it was periodically kept
informed of "advances in economic convergence." As for national parliaments, which had featured in the first draft of the Maastricht Treaty
in rather vague terms ("Governments shall bring the results of multilateral surveillance to the attention of their national parliaments"), they
duly vanished in the course of the negotiations.

A choir of voices expressed alarm at this in the European Parliament,
directly linking marginalization of the representative body to the absence
of a social and ecological dimension in European economic policies. As
early as 1990, in the first of a long series of parliamentary reports
tending to involve the EP in the drafting of BEPGs, the Liberal Pat Cox
had proposed that "the work of the Council in multilateral surveillance
should be prepared by the Monetary Committee, *in consultation* with

the Economic, Monetary and Industrial Policy Commission" of the European Parliament.[16] No success. A few months later, in his report of October 10, 1990, that would serve as a basis during the Maastricht negotiations, the Belgian federalist Fernand Herman, coming from the ranks of the European People's Party (EPP), proposed in his turn that the Commission's guidelines on multiannual economic policies and accompanying social policies "should be adopted by the Council in a joint decision with the European Parliament, after consultation with the Economic and Social Committee." So, once again it was clearly a question of bringing Parliament back into the EMU cockpit. But this was not to happen.

The European Parliament, supranational by construction, has never managed to adapt its monitoring to a system of multilateral surveillance still marked by an intergovernmental approach. Even today it intervenes too little and too late: it does not receive key documents such as national convergence programs, stability programs, or draft budgets that member states send to the European Commission in the framework of the European Semester (see Box 1). Above all, it lacks decision-making powers, participating neither in the establishment of the European Semester's strategic priorities, nor in the drafting of Country-Specific Recommendations (CSRs) once they have been adopted by the Council. In essence, European Parliament is confined to procedures of information, dialogue, and consultation—which again places parliamentarians in a passive position. And this is not to mention the Parliament's very limited powers of scrutiny over the Eurogroup—as the Eurogroup leaders have not failed to underline again recently by taking no account of the strong reservations expressed by the EP over the appointment of Luis de Guidos from Spain to the post of ECB vice president.[17] As for the European Stability Mechanism and the European Financial Stability Facility, which are key financial structures for the memorandums, they completely pass the EP by.

The national parliaments hardly come out of it better. As we know, the parliaments of countries that have benefited from financial assistance (Cyprus, Greece, Ireland, Portugal, Spain) have had their budgetary options severely restricted by the hasty adoption of an unamended series of structural reforms. It is worth recalling that, under the Greek adjustment program adopted by the Euro Summit on July 12, 2015, the Greek Parliament had one week to enact a package of unprecedented reforms con-

cerning pensions, taxes, civil courts, and so on. Hit in their core prerogatives, national parliaments have not remained idle and have geared up in
their turn. But this rearmament is still a long way from offsetting the loss
of control that results from the increased power of the European system
of economic and budgetary policy surveillance. The capacity of national
parliaments to influence the course of EMU policies is very weak or
close to zero. Most are content to be involved through consultation or
discussion with their government—often after the event, when the
government has already drawn up its annual plan for the Stability Pact.
In fact, if parliaments have tried to follow the process, it has been by
accepting a weak version of their powers of review (again the triad:
information, consultation, and debate),[18] which they are all the more
hesitant to use because governments frequently call on their "sense
of national responsibility." Parliaments have indeed tried to combine
forces in the modest Interparliamentary Conference created by the Fiscal
Compact. But this lacks binding powers and is a prisoner to conflicts between its European and national components; it has remained to this
day no more than a discussion forum, and it is hard to perceive in it any
policy-making potential.

Such, then, is the "democratic black hole" of this governance of the
euro: too Europeanized to be effectively controlled by each of the national parliaments, it remains too intergovernmental to be effectively
controlled by the European Parliament. Although here and there a
few scattered mechanisms orchestrate the role of parliaments, representative politics enters the picture—if at all—only at the end of the road,
to be consulted at best over choices and decisions deliberated in its
absence.

4. In Search of a Democratic Multiplier

In sum, the euro has had the effect of a constituent power on Europe.
Far from being just one more European community, the Economic and
Monetary Union is progressively imposing itself as a *cornerstone* for all
EU economic and social policies, and its restrictive effects are today
directly felt at the heart of national social pacts. Constructed by the
powerful network of national and European financial bureaucracies
around the objectives of financial stability, budgetary consolidation, and

structural reforms, this government has acquired considerable clout over the years and clamps member states' policies (budget, welfare, education, labor market) within a vise of common obligations and constraints. Through these multiple national ramifications, this new European power has definitively shattered what was left of the frontiers between the "European" level and the "national" level. Breaking with the European tradition of "gradualism," it has taken on the eminently *constrictive* power of political and administrative tutelage over member states "under program," to which social and budgetary shock therapies have been applied.

This powerful system of governance has developed *extra muros,* however, in an unmonitored space between the politics of member states and the politics of the European Union. Under the impact of the autonomized network of treasury departments and central banks, a "technocratic temptation" (to quote Pierre Moscovici) has progressively asserted itself. A whole policy of "containment" has thus helped to keep the actors of representative politics at a safe distance from the loci of decision making about the euro, to the point where, given the "burning obligation" of eurozone stability, votes are made to appear as so many intolerable "risks" and "uncertainties." In short, under the growing empire of this governance, the "off camera" area of democratic politics has been ceaselessly expanding.

At both the national and the EU level, then, the euro has helped to reinforce the structural subordination of parliaments, but also of social state players, in the steering of economic policies. Worse: it has developed a type of deafness—to the alarm signals coming from heterodox economists, to warnings from the European Committee of Social Rights, and to NGOs concerned with human rights (to take but a few examples). Entirely centered on the objectives of financial stability and improved public accounts, it has haughtily ignored alternative policy suggestions that would have made it possible to address long-term European integration, whether through an investment program in favor of European public goods, the networking of public investment banks, the reinsurance of national unemployment insurance schemes, and so forth. Obsessed with deviations from the budgetary norm, it has presented a united front against a series of modest attempts to renegotiate and reorient European economic policies, thereby blocking all prospects of significant policy change. And it is jointly responsible for the profound indifference to Brussels now felt by European citizens coming either from the popular or the middle classes, who are convinced that politicians are incapable of affecting the course of the policies developed there. It should not be forgotten that this political vacuum around the governance of the euro has been filled by far-right populist parties, which, for their part, have succeeded in imposing a transnational framework on the European crises of the past decade in terms of welfare nationalism and a rejection of European solidarity.

Consequently, the issue cannot be simply to inject a "dose" of democracy. We cannot be satisfied with the modest technical adjustments proposed in the imposing literature of reports, road maps, and assorted memorandums, which aim to "fix the Euro" and ritually appeal—in formulas whose imprecise terminology rivals their vague objectives—for the "strengthening of democratic government," "greater involvement" of national parliaments, and so on. The challenge is of an entirely different order. To leave the universe of democratic eclipses, it cannot be enough to think of a parliament as a body that ratifies deliberations and decisions taken elsewhere in its absence.

The T-Dem proposes, on the contrary, a real democratic transplant at the heart of this new European power bloc. The issue is not simply democratic in the institutional sense of the term—even if it is important, of course, to build the instruments that can wrest it from the opacity and the juridical-political unaccountability in which it has gradually taken refuge. To loosen the technocratic vise is also to make other policy choices possible; the (opaque and irresponsible) form of this governance of the euro and the (orthodox, narrowly financial) content of the policies forged within it are closely bound up with each other. In this sense, the democratic question is not only a question of democracy. By restoring the full importance of social mobilizations and transnational political divisions, one brings into the steering of the euro and the definition of European economic policies a number of players and causes that have hitherto been thoroughly excluded.

This is the *democratic multiplier,* which, in giving every chance to the transnational politics of parties and citizens, ought to release a breath of wind over the whole machinery of governance of the euro. The T-Dem, then, is not simply a reactive or defensive proposal to enable the formation of a democratic counterpower. By giving the euro a legislative and budgetary arm over which the Parliamentary Assembly thereby created will have the final say, it offers the necessary instruments for the formation of common policies of social and fiscal harmonization and for the launching of public investment that European citizens need today. Similarly, in registering how "national" and "European" have become blurred over the last two decades in connection with the euro, it offers a political framework to go beyond the lazy opposition between federalism and sovereignty and to avoid blockages and immobility linked to the Europe of national interests. In this sense, it is also a proposal for *effective* policies in the service of economic and social cohesion.

Bibliographical Note

This narrative of a "euro-ization of Europe" in part draws upon a set of investigations conducted over the years by the authors of the T-Dem; but it is also grounded in a rich body of literature in history, political economy, political science, and law that developed as the Economic and Monetary Union (EMU) was taking shape. This Bibliographical Note should thus be viewed, not as an exhaustive literature review, but instead as a list of intellectual debts owed while this text was being written.

The history of the EMU has long been a matter for insiders. Through the oral records of the Historical Archives of the EU and testimonies, the negotiators of the various European agreements and the members of expert committees have played a crucial role in constructing the narrative for the emergence of the euro. This has been so most notably for the "Maastricht moment" with, among others, the long essay by L. Bini-Smaghi, T. Padoa-Schioppa, and F. Papadia (1994), all three of whom are former members of the research department of the Banca d'Italia and prominent figures in the history of the euro area. The advisor to the director of the economic department of the DG ECFIN, Alexander Italianer also authored an excellent account of the context and conditions that brought about the famous "Maastricht (convergence) criteria" within the Monetary Committee (Italianer 1993). Other observers, such as Bernard Conolly (2011), who was in charge of European monetary policy within the Commission until he resigned in 1995, and the former

Greek finance minister Yanis Varoufakis (2017), offer a more critical approach, which conversely reflects their status as outsiders in the world of European economic governance (Lebaron and Georgakakis 2018).

It is only later, in the early 2000s, that the history of the EMU truly penetrated the academic field. The publication of the indispensable 800-page volume by Kenneth Dyson and Kevin Featherstone (1999) played a key role in this normalization process. Based on 280 interviews, this magnum opus offers a refined account of the "micro-decisions" that paved the way to the EMU, providing a story "from below"—which not only considers the key political negotiators of the EMU, but also focuses on those in the shadows, such as senior officials from national diplomatic services and finance ministries, central bankers, and European officials from the DG ECFIN. As shown by the specific case of Italy, the advent of the euro was also precipitated by national political and administrative elites, who imposed this "vincolo esterno" to strengthen their position in the domestic field of power (Dyson and Featherstone 1996). A few American studies, drawing upon intergovernmentalist theories, have also focused on the Franco-German deal as a key factor in the emergence of the EMU (see, for example, Moravcsik 1998; Howarth 2001), while others chose to emphasize the entrepreneurship of the Commission (Jabko 1999; Verdun 1999).

Confirming the normalization process, numerous empirical studies have investigated policy arenas that grand narratives had so far overlooked. The bureaucratic depths of the EMU were thus progressively delved into. Historian Harold James (2012) draws on historical archives from central banks and the Bank for International Settlements to shed light on the negotiations between central bankers (see also E. Mourlon-Druol 2012; Scheller 2011). Others have investigated the decisive contributions of central bankers (Maes 2012; Feiertag 2013; Lebaron 2016), senior officials from national treasuries (Lemoine 2016), certain academic circles (Buchner 2016; Helgadóttir 2016), the Delors Committee (Verdun 1999; Marcussen 2000), the Economic and Financial Committee (Verdun 2000), and the activity of the Eurogroup (see the pioneering work in Puetter 2006).

The economic and financial crisis, and the many new instruments it brought about in the field of economic and fiscal policy surveillance and coordination, have completed the normalization of this field of study.

An inquiry into the effects of these new policies has contributed to the understanding of the Stability and Growth Pact (Heipertz and Verdun 2004), the Broad Economic Policy Guidelines (Deroose, Hodson, and Kuhlmann 2008), the European Semester, and the adjustment programs entered into by states under financial assistance. Most notably, significant studies were conducted, in the framework of the research network Enlighten at the Free University of Brussels (Coman 2018; Crespy and Vanheuverzwijn 2017, 2018), on the many new arenas of political and administrative negotiations opened by these new procedures. We should also mention the work of lawyers (such as Dawson 2015; Dawson, Enderlein, and Joerges 2016), and others whose work was very valuable when writing this chapter, on the conditions leading up to the establishment of the government of the euro area (Dermine 2018) and the minor role played by social rights and, more generally, fundamental rights in that framework (Dermine and Schutter 2017). Last but not least, the observed emergence of a strong power center around the government of the euro area has raised questions about its consequences in terms of political accountability and democratic control, both at the European and national level. A rich set of studies by experts on parliamentarism around Nicola Lupo and Cristina Fasone (2016) from LUISS, but also by Ben Crum (2017) and Diane Fromage (2018) have highlighted the resulting political and democratic deficit (see also Scharpf 2015; Vauchez 2016).

As the study of European economic governance became a "normal" terrain of research, it was in turn deeply marked by the *summa divisio* in European studies between "intergovernmentalists" and "supranationalists." While the former argue that the management of the eurozone crisis has contributed to opening a new phase in the history of the Union established by the Maastricht Treaty (Bickerton, Hodson, and Puetter 2015), the latter observe a continuous consolidation of the position occupied, in the field of economic governance, by the Commission and the ECB (Dehousse 2016) and the network of institutions (such as Eurostat) that they coordinate (Savage 2005). Seeking to overcome the difficulties and many dead angles created by such opposition, a more relational and structuralist approach (Lebaron and Georgakakis 2018a, 2018b; Mudge and Vauchez 2016, 2018) has emphasized the interdependencies that cut across the different actors, institutions, and levels that make up this emerging transnational policy field.

—Translated by Patrick Camiller

Notes

1. "At EC, Gnomes in Shadows. Who Sets Monetary Policy? Try to Find Out," *International Herald Tribune,* October 24, 1992, quoted in Age F. P. Bakker, *The Liberalization of Capital Movements in Europe, the Monetary Committee and Financial Integration* (Dordrecht: Springer, 1996), 77.

2. Amy Verdun, "The Role of the Delors Committee in the Creation of EMU: An Epistemic Community?," *Journal of European Public Policy* 6, no. 2 (1999): 308–328.

3. Michael Buchner, "Forger un 'consensus schizophrène': Les économistes du cercle de Robert Triffin et les débats sur la réforme du système monétaire européen au début des années 80," *Revue économique* 67 (2016): 21.

4. Francesco Giavazzi and Marco Pagano, "The Advantage of Tying One's Hands: EMS Discipline and Central Bank Credibility," *European Economic Review* 32, no. 5 (1988): 1055–1082.

5. ECOFIN Council Declaration, December 1997.

6. Quoted in: Dermot Hodsen, "The ECB and the New Intergovernmentalism," in *The New Intergovernmentalism: States and Supranational Actors in the Post-Maastricht Era,* ed. Christopher Bickerton, Dermot Hodson, and Uwe Puetter (Oxford: Oxford University Press, 2015).

7. Jan-Werner Müller, "Rule-Breaking," *London Review of Books,* August 7, 2015, 3–7.

8. EU Ombudsman to Eurogroup President, March 14, 2016; Eurogroup President to EU Ombudsman, May 16, 2016, https://www.ombudsman.europa.eu/en/correspondence/en/48285 and 67821.

9. ECOFIN Council, 90 / 141 / CEE, March 12, 1990.

10. Directive 121 / 74 / CEE, February 18, 1974.

11. In the case of France, for example, these recommendations included bringing the budget deficit below the threshold of 3% of GDP, encouraging participation in an active life, reducing structural unemployment, ensuring the long-term viability of public finances in the face of demographic ageing, ensuring competition in network industries, and accelerating measures to create a level playing field in the internal market.

12. Uwe Puetter, *The Eurogroup: How a Secretive Circle of Finance Ministers Shapes European Economic Governance* (Manchester: Manchester University Press, 2006).

13. James D. Savage, *Making the EMU: The Politics of Budgetary Surveillance and the Enforcement of Maastricht* (Oxford: Oxford University Press, 2005).

14. Kenneth Dyson and Kevin Featherstone, "Italy and EMU as a 'Vincolo Esterno': Empowering the Technocrats, Transforming the State," *South European Society and Politics* 1, no. 2 (1996): 272–299.

15. Susana Borras and Kerstin Jacobsson, "The Open Method of Co-Ordination and the New Governance Patterns in the EU," *Journal of European Public Policy* 11, no. 2 (2004): 185–208.
16. Doc. A 3-21 / 90.
17. "Démocratiser l'Europe commence à la Banque central européenne", *Le Monde*, January 22, 2018.
18. Ben Crum, "Parliamentary Accountability in Multilevel Governance: What Role for Parliaments in Post-Crisis EU Economic Governance?," *Journal of European Public Policy* 25, no. 2 (2017): 268–286.

Bibliography

Bakker, A. 1996. *The Liberalization of Capital Movements in Europe, the Monetary Committee and Financial Integration, 1958–1994*. Dordrecht: Springer, 1996.

Bickerton, C., D. Hodson, and U. Puetter, eds. 2015. *The New Intergovernmentalism: States and Supranational Actors in the Post-Maastricht Era*. Oxford: Oxford University Press.

Bini-Smaghi, L., T. Padoa-Schioppa, and F. Papadia. 1994. "The Transition to EMU in the Maastricht Treaty." Essays in International Finance, no. 194. Department of Economics, Princeton University.

Blyth, M. 2013. *Austerity: The History of a Dangerous Idea*. Oxford: Oxford University Press.

Buchner, M. 2016. "Forger un 'consensus schizophrène': Les économistes du cercle de Robert Triffin et les débats sur la réforme du système monétaire européen au début des années 80," *Revue économique* 67:21.

Coman, R. 2018. "Who Gets What and How in the European Semester? Large and Small Member States in the Coordination of Macroeconomic Policies at the EU level." Paper presented at the Council for European Studies, March 28–31, Chicago.

Conolly, B. 2012. *The Rotten Heart of Europe: The Dirty War for Europe's Money*. London: Faber and Faber.

Crespy, A., and P. Vanheuverzwijn. 2017. "What 'Brussels' Means by Structural Reforms: Empty Signifier or Constructive Ambiguity?" *Comparative European Politics*, https://doi.org/10.1057/s41295-017-0111-0.

———. 2018. "Macro-Economic Coordination and Elusive Ownership in the European Union." *Public Administration* 96 (3):578–593.

Crum, B. 2017. "Parliamentary Accountability in Multilevel Governance: What Role for Parliaments in Post-Crisis EU Economic Governance?" *Journal of European Public Policy* 25 (2): 268–286.

Dawson, M. 2015. "The Legal and Political Accountability Structure of 'Post-Crisis' EU Economic Governance." *Journal of Common Market Studies* 53 (5):976–993.

Dawson, M., H. Enderlein, and C. Joerges, eds. 2016. *Beyond the Crisis: The Governance of Europe's Economic, Political and Legal Transformation.* Oxford: Oxford University Press.

Dehousse, R. 2016. "Why Has EU Macroeconomic Governance Become More Supranational?" *Journal of European Integration* 38 (5):617–631.

Dermine, P. 2018. "European Economic Governance in Post-Crisis Era." *European Papers* 3 (1):281–306.

Dermine, P., and Olivier De Schutter. 2017. "The Two Constitutions of Europe." *Journal européen des droits de l'homme,* no. 2, 108–156.

Deroose, S., D. Hodson , and J. Kuhlmann. 2008. "The Broad Economic Policy Guidelines: Before and after the Re-Launch of the Lisbon Strategy." *Journal of Common Market Studies* 46 (4):827–848.

Dyson, K., and K. Featherstone. 1996. "Italy and EMU as a 'Vincolo Esterno': Empowering the Technocrats, Transforming the State." *South European Society and Politics* 1 (2):272–299.

———. 1999. *The Road to Maastricht: Negotiating Economic and Monetary Union.* Oxford: Oxford University Press.

Fasone, C. 2014. "European Economic Governance and Parliamentary Representation: What Place for the European Parliament?" *European Law Journal* 20 (2):164–185.

Feiertag, O. 2013. *Wilfried Baumgartner: Un grand commis des finances à la croisée des pouvoirs (1902–1978).* Institut de la gestion publique et du développement économique.

Fromage, D. 2018. "Les parlements nationaux: Des acteurs européens en devenir?" *Politique européenne,* no. 59, 9–22.

Heipertz, M., and A. Verdun. 2004. "The Dog That Would Never Bite? What We Can Learn from the Origins of Stability and Growth Pact." *Journal of European Public Policy* 11 (5):765–780.

Helgadóttir, O. 2016. "The Bocconi Boys Go to Brussels: Italian Economic Ideas, Professional Networks and European Austerity." *Journal of European Public Policy* 23 (3):392–409.

Howarth, D. 2001. *The French Road to European Monetary Union.* Basingstoke, UK: Palgrave.

Italianer, A. 1993. "Mastering Maastricht: EMU Issues and How They Were Settled." In *Economic and Monetary Union: Implications for National Policy-Makers,* edited by Klaus Gretschmann, 51–113. Dordrecht: Martinus Nijhoff.

Jabko, N. 1999. "In the Name of the Market: How the European Commission Paved the Way for Monetary Union." *Journal of European Public Policy* 6 (3):475–495.

James, H. 2012. *Making the European Monetary Union.* Cambridge, MA: Harvard University Press.

Kees, A. 1994. "The Monetary Committee as a Promoter of European Integra-tion." In *Monetary Stability through International Cooperation: Essays in*

Honour of André Szasz, edited by A. Bakker, H. Boot, O. Sleijpen, and W. Vanthoor. Dordrecht: Kluwer Academic.

Lebaron, F. 2016. "Do Central Bankers' Biographies Matter?" *Sociologica* 10 (2).

Lebaron, F., and D. Georgakakis. 2018a, forthcoming. "The European Economic Austerity and the Field of the European Economic Governance." *Global Networks.*

———. 2018b, "Yanis Varoufakis, the Minotaure and the Field of Eurocracy." *Historical Social Research.*43 (3):216–248.

Lemoine, B. 2016. *L'ordre de la dette: Enquête sur les infortunes de l'état et la prospérité du marché.* Paris: La Découverte.

Lupo, N., and C. Fasone, eds. 2018. *Interparliamentary Cooperation in the Composite European Constitution.* Oxford: Hart.

Maes, I. 2012. "Tommaso Padoa-Schioppa and the Origins of the Euro." Working Paper no. 222, National Bank of Belgium.

Marcussen, M. 2000. *Ideas and Elites: The Social Construction of Economic and Monetary Union.* Aalborg: Aalborg University Press.

Moravcsik, A. 1998. *The Choice for Europe: Social Purpose and State Power from Messina to Maastricht.* Ithaca, NY: Cornell University Press.

Mourlon-Druol, E. 2012. *A Europe Made of Money: The Emergence of the European Monetary System.* Ithaca, NY: Cornell University Press.

Mudge S., and A. Vauchez, 2013. « State-building on a Weak Field. Law, Economics and the Scholarly Production of Europe», *American Journal of Sociology,* 118 (2):449–492

Mudge, S., and A. Vauchez. 2016. "Fielding Supranationalism: The European Central Bank, Hyper-Scientization, and the Logic of Field Effects." *Sociological Review,* https://doi.org/10.1002/2059-7932.12006.

Pisani-Ferry, J. 2006. "Only One Bed for Two Dreams: A Critical Retrospective on the Debate over the Economic Governance of the Euro Area." *Journal of Common Market Studies* 44 (4):823–844.

Puetter, U. 2006. *The Eurogroup: How a Secretive Circle of Finance Ministers Shapes European Economic Governance.* Manchester: Manchester University Press.

Sandholtz, W. 1996. "Money Troubles: Europe's Rough Road to Monetary Union." *Journal of European Public Policy* 3 (1):84–101.

Savage, J. D. 2005. *Making the EMU: The Politics of Budgetary Surveillance and the Enforcement of Maastricht.* Oxford: Oxford University Press.

Scharpf, F. 2015. *Political Legitimacy in a Non-Optimal Currency Area.* MPIfG Discussion Paper 13 / 15, Max-Planck-Institut für Gesellschaftsforschung, Cologne.

Scheller, H. 2011. "Le comité des gouverneurs des banques centrales de la CEE et l'unification monétaire européenne." *Histoire, Économie et Société,* no. 4, 79–99.

Tooze, A. 2018. *Crashed: How a Decade of Financial Crises Changed the World.* Viking: New York.

Varoufakis, Y. 2017. *Adults in the Room: My Battle with Europe's Deep Establishment.* London: Bodley Head.

Vauchez, A. 2016. *Democratizing Europe.* Basingstoke, UK: Palgrave.

Verdun, A. 1999. "The Role of the Delors Committee in the Creation of EMU: An Epistemic Community?" *Journal of European Public Policy* 6 (2):308–328

———. 2000. "Governing by Committee: The Case of Monetary Policy." In *Committee Governance in the European Union,* edited by T. Christiansen and E. Kirchner, 132–144. Manchester: Manchester University Press.

2

On the Legal Feasibility of a Treaty to Democratize the Governance of the Euro Area

Can the member states of the European Union whose currency is the euro conclude an international treaty determining democratic procedures applicable to the eurozone without conflicting with the obligations they have incurred by virtue of belonging to the Union (such has respect for European treaties, for the powers accorded to the Union, and for the principle of loyal cooperation)?

This question must, without any doubt, be answered in the affirmative, for at least three series of reasons:

1. In 2012 the Court of Justice of the European Union (CJEU) ruled that the acceptance by a member state of the Treaty Establishing the European Stability Mechanism (ESM) did not contravene the obligations resulting, for that country, from the treaties on which the European Union is founded; this reasoning can be applied to the question of the feasibility of a treaty to democratize the eurozone.

2. The proposal for reform that consists of making the Parliamentary Assembly of the Euro Area an institution of the "governance of the euro area" does not infringe on the functioning of the institutions of the EU because it does not take any competence away from them. In fact, because they actually involve the institutions of the Union, the new procedures defined by the T-Dem

are a pledge of respect for the principles on which the Union is
founded.

3. Lastly, there is no other legal path, particularly within the
framework of the EU treaties, that permits the same result to be
attained.

These three points are developed below.

1. In the *Pringle* case adjudicated in 2012, the Court of Justice was
directly confronted with a question very similar to the one raised by the
proposed T-Dem: Can an international treaty (at the time, the ESM
Treaty) be validly concluded by the member states of the European
Union without their ignoring the obligations they have contracted vis-
à-vis the Union? The Court answered in the affirmative, by developing
the following reasoning, which we suggest can be extended with regard
to the T-Dem (CJEU, 27 November 2012, *Thomas Pringle v Government of
Ireland,* C-370 / 12).

In its *Pringle* decision the Court first established that the ESM Treaty
did not alter the exclusive competence of the EU in monetary policy. Article 3§1c of the Treaty on the Functioning of the European Union
(TFEU) stipulates in fact that the Union enjoys exclusive competence in
the field of monetary policy for those member states whose currency is
the euro. Accordingly, as the Court explains clearly (§§53 and 54 of the
decision), the TFEU does not contain any definition of monetary policy
and refers essentially to its objectives. It further indicates that these primarily consist of "maintaining price stability," by virtue of articles 127§1
and 282§2 of the TFEU.

Subsequently, the Court upheld the possibility for EU member states
that belong to the eurozone to conclude a treaty creating a "European
Stability Mechanism": Despite the fact that the establishment of such a
mechanism could indirectly have repercussions on the stability of the
euro, this would not be a matter of a "monetary policy" in the sense of
article 3§1 of the TFEU. Further, the Court added that because the competence of the EU in economic policies is essentially one of coordination,
it is not infringed by states' decision to establish a stability mechanism.
Furthermore, along those lines a second treaty, signed in March 2012
and similarly parallel to the EU treaties, imposes the golden budgetary
rule that the Commission and the Court of Justice are involved in
guaranteeing. Based on what it determined with respect to the ESM,

had it been invited to rule on the admissibility of such a "budgetary pact" the Court of Justice would most likely have upheld it: neither of these mechanisms alter the functioning and the competences of the EU.

It can be assumed that this line of reasoning of the Court pertaining to the compatibility between a treaty concluded within the eurozone (the ESM Treaty) and the allocation of competences between the Union and its member states as determined by the EU treaties can be taken up *a fortiori* with regard to the T-Dem. The Court of Justice has indeed ruled that the compatibility of the ESM Treaty with the EU Treaties rests (at least in part) on the fact that the objective of the ESM is not to maintain price stability, but merely to satisfy the financing needs of ESM members (who are, by definition, member states whose currency is the euro). Within that framework, it appears that the T-Dem, which does not materially affect any exclusive competence and concerns only shared competences (economic coordination), and whose range is primarily institutional (improvement of the democratic standards of the eurozone), does not infringe on the obligations contracted by the EU member states.

The Court also established that, because the ESM Treaty does not alter the exclusive competence of the EU in monetary policy, the states can choose to establish, by way of international treaty, mechanisms of stability governing the eurozone without impairing the competences of the EU. Applied to the T-Dem, this reasoning can be extended in the following way: Because the contracting parties to the ESM Treaty could validly create the institution called the "European Stability Mechanism" in order to reinforce the Economic and Monetary Union, they are necessarily founded to create a Parliamentary Assembly of the Euro Area with a view to improving the procedures governing the functioning of said zone. Indeed, because the ESM Treaty was interpreted as not affecting or not calling into question any competence of the EU, a similar argument can be made for the T-Dem treaty, whose substantial innovations are clearly less important. The signatory states of the T-Dem are thus to be deemed empowered to conclude such a treaty that does not impair the exclusive competences of the European Union with regard to monetary policy.

It is thus argued that the conclusion and the ratification by the states whose currency is the euro of a T-Dem guaranteeing the democratically responsible nature of the institutions in charge of the governance of the eurozone do not prevent the EU from exercising its own competences in the defense of the common interest.

2. Further, the procedures that elevate the Parliamentary Assembly of the Euro Area to the rank of a governing institution of the eurozone do not impair the functioning of the institutions of the European Union, from which they do not take any competence away. In fact, because they involve the institutions of the Union, the new procedures defined by the T-Dem are a pledge of respect for the principles on which the law of the Union is founded.

Because no provision of the EU treaties endows the Union with exclusive competence in the field of the internal economic policy of the eurozone, the member states are empowered to act in this domain. At any rate, this is the reasoning on the basis of which they have successively adopted, parallel to EU treaties, the ESM Treaty, and the Treaty on Stability, Coordination and Governance (TSCG). The T-Dem institutes a Parliamentary Assembly of the Euro Area. It also determines the procedures of collaboration between the Assembly and the other competent institutions at the eurozone level—notably, the Euro Summits (the councils of the heads of state) and the Eurogroup (the council of the ministers of the eurozone). In doing so, the T-Dem in no way disrupts the institutional equilibrium of the European Union, because its sphere of action is not that of the European Union but merely that of the eurozone; and what affects the latter does not alter the former. This also results from further case-law of the Court that has clearly ruled that the ESM is not an EU institution and that an appeal made against a declaration of the Eurogroup related to assistance granted in the framework of the ESM was inadmissible (CJEU, 20 September 2015, *Konstantinos Mallis v Commission and BCE*, C-105/15 and C-10-9/15).

The T-Dem also determines procedures of collaboration of the Parliamentary Assembly of the Euro Area with certain institutions of the European Union (the European Parliament and the European Central Bank, notably). But there, too, it does so operating in the wake of what has been ruled by the Court of Justice. In the *Pringle* decision, the Court has precisely determined that "the Member States are entitled, in areas which do not fall under the exclusive competence of the Union, to entrust tasks to the institutions, outside the framework of the Union" (§158). Thus, the T-Dem neither affects nor alters the missions entrusted to the EU institutions (compare §161 of the *Pringle* decision). It can thus be deemed compatible with the EU treaties.

3. Lastly, the existing institutional framework does not allow for the end result pursued by the T-Dem to be achieved.

As things stand, the provisions of the treaties related to the European Union (the Treaty on European Union, and the TFEU) do not grant the Union any specific competence to establish a mechanism of democratic control comparable to the one the embodied by the T-Dem. In this sense, the framework of the EU treaties is not suited to achieving the goals they pursue. The T-Dem aims not to complement the institutional framework of the EU; even less so does it call it into question. Its goal is to create, through the creation of a Parliamentary Assembly of the Euro Area, an institution responsible for the governance of the eurozone, together with the gathering of the heads of state and government whose currency is the euro (the Euro Summit) as well as the gathering of the council of the economy and finance ministers of the states whose currency is the euro (the Eurogroup). It is situated on a plane different from that of EU institutions. What it does complement is the setup that results from the TSCG for the governance of the eurozone (item V of the TSCG). Hence the inappropriateness of the EU treaties, which do not provide an appropriate legal basis on which to pursue a goal to democratize the euro area.

As for article 13 of the TSCG: it certainly defines the role of the European Parliament and the national parliaments of the contracting parties "in the organization and promotion of a conference . . . to discuss budgetary policies and other issues covered by this Treaty." It cannot, however, be taken as a sufficiently firm basis on which to elevate an institution exercising legislative power and political control within the framework of the governance of the eurozone.

Finally, notwithstanding the fact that the legal framework of the European Union envisages "enhanced cooperation" mechanisms that allow a group of member states to go forward in determined areas of action, this framework would not lend itself well to the project that underlies the proposed T-Dem. With regard to the areas of intervention considered within the eurozone (economic, fiscal, social policy), the deployment of a logic of enhanced cooperation would necessarily lead to depriving the national parliaments of the powers that are granted to them by the constitution.

Is law a combat sport? Without necessarily providing a final answer to that question, one can borrow from aikido an essential principle that exemplifies the working principle of the proposed T-Dem: one must lean on the strength of the adversary.

The adversary here is multiple: ESM, TSCG, Six-Pack, Two-Pack, and so on—in brief, and without developing here a long series of acronyms that is explained elsewhere in this book, it is a whole system of governance of the eurozone that has emerged through the political and institutional responses that were hastily drafted to deal with the crisis of sovereign debts. It is indeed an "adversary" because this piling on of measures has engendered an informal and opaque but genuine power structure that has contributed to consolidating an economic policy of austerity in the Union (and this occurred at the very moment when austerity was being abandoned elsewhere—on the other side of Atlantic, for example). Yet it is a strong adversary. These responses to the crisis of the eurozone have revealed the wide range of possibilities that exist beside and outside the EU treaties themselves that many deem to be untouchable.

This has led to a regrettable state of affairs. The institutional framework of the European treaties, patiently constructed over the course of six decades of European integration, does indeed offer a number of guarantees (transparency, political pluralism, fundamental rights). However, ten years after the painful birth of the last European treaty (the Lisbon Treaty signed in 2007) and in a context in which "illiberal democracies" are emerging at the very heart of the EU (Hungary, Poland), it seems that no one today envisages the possibility of reopening the Herculean labor of revising treaties that tie twenty-seven member states together.

The T-Dem explores another path and proposes a concrete perspective of rapid political change. Starting from the observation that both the Treaty Establishing the European Stability Mechanism and the TSCG came into existence outside of and parallel to the EU treaties framework, and that this form of circumvention of the EU treaties was justified, both times, in the name of the economic and financial emergency caused by the crisis of the euro (and even upheld by the European Court of Justice, as explained above), the T-Dem proposal chooses to follow a similar path with a view to confronting the existing European democratic emergency. In sum, the proposal is to walk the same path (adoption of an international treaty not within the EU legal framework but within the parallel legal framework of the eurozone). It does so, however, with the objective of attaining very different ends—in this case, the democratization of the governance of the eurozone. The proposed scheme also allows the integration of a number of institutions, such as the Euro Summits and the Eurogroup, whose existence and competence have so far been established in a mostly informal way. This, of course, is essential in order to make them both accountable and responsible.

The T-Dem, in sum, emerges in the wake of the ESM Treaty and the TSCG, but with the goals of correcting their logic and democratizing their terms. By doing so, it expresses the idea that the treaties' "marble" is not as hard as is often a bit lazily affirmed—provided there exists sufficient political will to reorient the European project. The T-Dem is also, simultaneously, a serious proposal: the democratic urgency before us will not be honored with superficial talk and ritual evocations of a necessary relaunching of the European project. The institution of a Parliamentary Assembly of the Euro Area—the T-Dem's core proposal aiming to establish the presence of European democratic forces at the heart of the governance of the eurozone—would only make sense if it were endowed with authentic competences: legislative power, power to control, and so forth. The elements explained in detail hereafter are thus intended to make explicit the reasoning and legal choices that underlie the T-Dem and to bring together the principal arguments supporting the thesis that democratizing the eurozone is indeed feasible.

—Translated by Marc LePain

– 3 –

What Would the Parliamentary Assembly of the Euro Area Look Like?

What would be the actual composition and political orientation of the Parliamentary Assembly of the Euro Area established by the Democratization Treaty? More than one scenario is conceivable, depending on whether the Assembly is restricted (around 100 members) or enlarged (the maximum of 400 members provided for in the T-Dem, art. 4).

In the case of a restricted Assembly, with a hypothetical 100 members coming from national parliaments, Germany would delegate 24 members (because it represents 24% of the eurozone population), France 20 members, Italy 18 members, Spain 14 members, and so forth. To guarantee a minimum of one seat for each member state (T-Dem, art. 4), there would have to be five additional seats—hence, a total of 105 members coming from national parliaments. If we then add 25 members coming from the European Parliament, we get a total of 130 members: 105 from national parliaments (80%) and 25 from the European Parliament (20%). This smaller Assembly would have the advantage of greater efficiency.

Conversely, an enlarged Assembly would mean that political plurality could be taken better into account, especially for small countries, which would obtain a minimum of three members. This would give an Assembly of 400 members, 320 coming from national parliaments and 80 from the European Parliament (see Table 1).

It is also possible to think of the eventual political composition of this Assembly on a left–right scale. There is something artificial in this, of

Table 1   Assembly of the Euro Area: Distribution of Seats by Country

	Population (millions) (Eurostat estimates on January 1, 2016)	Population (% of Euro Area)	Number of seats in the Assembly of the Euro Area	
			Version 1: Restricted Assembly (proportionate to population on a base of 100 seats, plus minimum of one seat for small countries, hence an assembly of 105 seats)	Version 2: Enlarged Assembly (number of seats tripled over restricted version)
Germany	82	24%	24	72
France	67	20%	20	60
Italy	61	18%	18	54
Spain	46	14%	14	42
Netherlands	17	5%	5	15
Belgium	11	3%	3	9
Greece	11	3%	3	9
Portugal	10	3%	3	9
Austria	9	3%	3	9
Finland	5	2%	2	6
Slovakia	5	2%	2	6
Ireland	5	1%	1	6
Lithuania	3	1%	1	5
Slovenia	2	1%	1	3
Latvia	2	1%	1	3
Estonia	1	0%	1	3
Cyprus	1	0%	1	3
Luxembourg	1	0%	1	3
Malta	0	0%	1	3
	340	100%	105	320
Representatives of European Parliament			25	80
Total members of Assembly			130	400

course, because the boundaries defining the "right," "left," and "extreme left" camps vary from country to country, and most often they struggle to exist as such in the setting of the EU. However, such political groupings and potential majorities indicate the possible shape of a truly transnational politics. This gives a real sense of what transnational parliamentary socialization around party identities and political divisions might cause to emerge, and how national lefts and rights might be redefined within this Assembly—especially if it proves to not be simply a rubber-stamping chamber but exercises effective powers.

Whichever solution is adopted, it should be noted that the composition of the Assembly would incline quite clearly to the left, at given the state of political groups present in the various national parliaments as of March 2017 (see Table 2). For example, on the hypothesis of a restricted Assembly, the 105 members coming from national parliaments

Table 2   Assembly of the Euro Area : Distribution of Seats among Political Groups (Members Coming from National Parliaments)

	Number of seats in Assembly of the Euro Area *(proportionate to population on a base of 100 seats, plus a minimum of one seat for small countries)*	Proportionate distribution of seats for political groups present in national parliaments (highest average) (February 2017)[1]			
		Right (CDU, LR, PP, etc.)	Left (SPD, Grünen, PS, PD, PSOE, etc.)	Radical Left (Die Linke, Podemos, Syriza, etc.)	Others (M5S, etc.)
Germany	24	12	10	2	0
France	20	9	11	0	0
Italy	18	3	12	0	3
Spain	14	7	4	3	0
Netherlands	5	2	2	1	0
Belgium	3	2	1	0	0
Greece	3	1	0	2	0
Portugal	3	1	1	1	0
Austria	3	1	1	0	1
Finland	2	1	0	0	1
Slovakia	2	1	1	0	0
Ireland	1	1	0	0	0
Lithuania	1	0	1	0	0
Slovenia	1	0	1	0	0
Latvia	1	0	1	0	0
Estonia	1	1	0	0	0
Cyprus	1	1	0	0	0
Luxembourg	1	1	0	0	0
Malta	1	0	1	0	0
Total	105	44	47	9	5

1. We have decided to keep the figures presented in table 2 as they were when the T-Dem was initially published, although it should be mentioned that left-wing parties have lost various important elections ever since.

would break down into 44 members from the extreme right and centre right (CDU / CSU, LR [Républicains], PP, and so on), 47 from the left and the ecologists (SPD, Greens, PS, PD, PSOE, and so on), 9 from the so-called radical left (Die Linke, Podemos, Syriza, and so on), and 5 unclassified (Five Stars Movement, and so on). This balance would change only marginally if taking into account the 25 members coming from the European Parliament in proportion to the various groups.[1]

It should also be noted that, on questions relating to budgetary policy, reflation of the European economy, debt restructuring, and so forth, the positions of the French, Spanish, or Italian right are often quite markedly different from those of the German right, which would have only 12 seats (out of the 105 members coming from national parliaments) within the Assembly of the Euro Area.

To sum up: The Parliamentary Assembly of the Euro Area is not a panacea; our proposed Treaty can and should be improved and completed; and we in no way claim that the decisions taken by this Assembly will always conform to our wishes or enable all the problems of Europe to be solved as if by magic. But it seems to us reasonable to say that this Assembly provides a democratic framework for making austerity a minority option, or at least for substantially altering the present power balance.

One last point: It may be worth noting that the results would hardly differ if the seats were distributed in proportion to the various countries' gross domestic product (GDP) rather than their population. Such an electoral system, which would mean applying a rule of "one euro, one vote" among countries, would evidently be less satisfactory from a democratic point of view, and in our eyes would be totally unacceptable. (Why not apply it also among regions, among individuals?) But the fact is that it would lead to very similar results for the composition of the Assembly, simply because per capita GDP is quite similar among countries within the eurozone. Concretely, Germany represents 24% of the eurozone population, compared with 51% for France, Italy, and Spain combined, and 25% for the other countries.[2] In other words, if we applied the GDP distribution key, the number of seats allocated to Germany would increase slightly, but the political balance would be only very marginally affected: for example, the German right would have 14 seats instead of 12 (out of 105 members coming from national parliaments).

—Translated by Patrick Camiller

Notes

1. Detailed simulations and the full data used here are available online at http://piketty.blog.lemonde.fr/2017/03/09/assemblee-de-la-zone-euro.
2. See http://piketty.blog.lemonde.fr/2017/03/09/assemblee-de-la-zone-euro for detailed tables available online.

– 4 –

What to Do if Some Member States Reject the Proposed Treaty?

L et us now tackle a delicate question: What will happen if some of our partners refuse to discuss the Treaty on the Democratization of the Governance of the Euro Area? To take a textbook case, what will happen if German political leaders, fearing to be in a minority in a democratic Assembly of the Euro Area, shut the door on any negotiation? Three sets of answers are possible.

First, even on the gloomiest hypothesis—that some of our partners will refuse any discussion—it seems essential to put a possible alternative on the table. Up to now, French political leaders have never proposed to their eurozone partners a real project for parliamentary and political union. France regularly complains about Brussels or Germany, sometimes about the whole world, but we have scarcely ever seen a clear public proposal that would allow a more democratic and more social Europe to be put in place. Even if worst comes to worst and our partners simply reject these proposals, the stage of presenting and explaining disagreements seems to us essential from a political and historical point of view. If France publicly proposed parliamentary democracy to the euro area and Germany—on the basis of one person, one vote—and if Germany stubbornly refused any discussion on such a proposal, this would probably result in a climate of mistrust and exasperation that would eventually get the better of the euro area. It is likely that other votes, in other elections in France and elsewhere, would lead to new exits and an explosion of the European project. But even in this extremely gloomy case, we think it essential that a plausible democratic alternative should have first been openly debated.

Second, this ultra-pessimistic scenario does not seem to us the most realistic—far from it. Our partners, especially our German partners, are at least as attached as we are to the values of parliamentary democracy and are often much more advanced in their reflections on political union. Apart from the fact that political power in Germany may well change hands and swing to the left in the near future, a large number of German citizens and political leaders, including on the right, would look very favorably on a French proposal for parliamentary union of the euro area. At the very least, there can be no doubt that negotiations would start up and that a compromise (the nature of which no one can prejudge) would have to be found. The pressure of peoples and opinions, especially in Italy and Spain, is pushing in the direction of the democratization of Europe.

Third, the T-Dem project itself, in its conditions for ratification (art. 20), envisages a possible way out of the crisis. If ten of the nineteen countries in the euro area, representing at least 70% of its population, ratified the T-Dem, this would be enough for it to come into force. Theoretically, it is possible to envisage its coming into force without its being ratified by one of the major countries—Germany, for example. That does not seem the most desirable or most probable path—far from it! But there is at least one way in which countries could show they are willing, if they wish to do so: they could launch a process of partial ratification as a way to increase the pressure on countries that refuse any discussion. The point today is not to set cutoff dates beyond which a Brexit game would begin. Rather, it is to suggest concrete actions that might show there is a democratic way out of the contradictions in which our continent is trapped.

—Translated by Patrick Camiller

PART TWO

DRAFT TREATY ON THE DEMOCRATIZATION OF THE GOVERNANCE OF THE EURO AREA (T-DEM)

– 5 –

Explanatory Statement

In addressing the crisis of the euro area, member states have built a "euro-area governance" system—including the Treaty on Stability, Coordination and Governance (TSCG); the Treaty Establishing the European Stability Mechanism (ESM); the Regulation on the Banking Union; and the "Six-Pack" and "Two-Pack" legislative packages. This has contributed to the consolidation of austerity policies across the economic and monetary union.

The significant strengthening of the executive capacity of European institutions in the field of economic policy has taken place in the absence of any parallel development of parliamentary control. The European Parliament is largely excluded from the governance of the euro area. Symptomatically, article 12§1 of the TSCG foresees that "the President of the European Central Bank shall be invited to take part" in the meetings of the heads of state or government of the euro area, but its article 12§5 merely provides that "the President of the European Parliament may be invited to be heard." As for the national parliaments, the TSCG only acknowledges their limited advisory power in its article 13— which refers to the protocol on the role of national parliaments in the European Union annexed to the European Union Treaties.

This imbalance deeply compromises the commitment of the EU heads of state and government broadly to "respect for and maintenance of representative democracy," which they solemnly declared to be an "essential element of membership" of the European Union in the Copenhagen Declaration of the European Council of April 8, 1978, and which they have constantly renewed since then. It also contradicts the status of democracy, under Articles 2 and 13 of the Treaty on European Union (TEU), as one of the "values" that the Union's institutions shall "promote."

As this deficit of democratic legitimacy increases European citizens' estrangement from the European project, it carries the risk of a breakup of the European Union. Five years ago, the establishment of the ESM was justified by the urgent need to address pressing issues of financial stability. Similarly today, we face a democratic emergency that calls for a revamping of the decision-making processes that structure the euro area.

In view of the interconnection between economic and monetary policies and the intertwinement of the European Union's and the member states' competences, only an overall revision of the European treaties could provide the euro area with the institutional framework it needs to overcome the original shortcomings of the Economic and Monetary Union.

However, as this option appears strongly impractical in the short term, the possible adoption, in a short time frame, of an international Treaty to Democratize the Governance of the Euro Area (hereinafter "T-Dem") signed by the member states whose currency is the euro, and which puts "democratic conditionality" at its core, shall be considered.

The objective of the present draft treaty is twofold. On the one hand, it seeks to guarantee that convergence and conditionality policies, which currently are at the heart of the governance of the euro area, are carried out by institutions that are democratically accountable, at both the European and the national levels. On the other hand, it allows that the next necessary steps—toward deepened fiscal and social convergence and economic and budgetary coordination within the euro area—will not be decided upon without the direct involvement of the representatives of national parliaments.

The Parliamentary Assembly of the Euro Area foreseen by the present draft treaty fully contributes to the governance of the euro area. Firstly, the Assembly sets the political agenda, by taking part in the preparation of the agenda of the Euro Summits (council of heads of state or government) as well as in the semiannual work program of the Eurogroup (council of ministers of the euro area). Secondly, the Assembly is endowed with a legislative capacity in order to foster economic and fiscal convergence as well as sustainable growth and employment. Thirdly, the

Assembly has the means to control the convergence and conditionality policies that have emerged over the past decade within the euro area; and in the case of a disagreement between the Assembly and the Eurogroup, the former has the final say on the euro-area budget, the base and rate of corporate tax, and any other legislative act foreseen by the T-Dem.

For this purpose, the present draft treaty seeks to maximize the legal margins of maneuver that could allow the creation of a truly democratic system of governance for the euro area, *as a complement to* the European Union treaties. In so doing, the T-Dem replicates the *modus operandi* of both the TSCG and the ESM Treaty (as validated by the Court of Justice of the European Union in its *Pringle* ruling from November 2012) to address the financial crisis, but does so in order to engage in a democratizing effort. It seeks to demonstrate that the European project is not cast "in stone"—provided there is enough political will to shift its orientation; and it affirms that the path of democratization of the governance of the euro area is worth following.

—Translated by Paul Dermine

6

Draft Treaty on the Democratization of the Governance of the Euro Area (T-Dem)

RESOLVED to reiterate, against a succession of economic, political, and social crises, the importance of the European integration process undertaken sixty years ago with the establishment of the European Communities,

CONSCIOUS of the need, recalled by Protocol No. 14 of the Lisbon Treaty, to "lay down special provisions for enhanced dialogue between the Member States whose currency is the euro,"

TAKING NOTICE of the political and institutional upheavals brought about by the financial crisis and the emergence of a true "governance of the euro area" to which a variety of institutions take part, in various capacities: the council of heads of state or government of the euro area (the "Euro Summit" as established by Article 12 of the Treaty on Stability, Coordination and Governance [TSCG]), the council of ministers of the euro area (the Eurogroup as recognized by Article 137 TFEU and Protocol No. 14 of the Lisbon Treaty), the European Commission, the Court of Justice of the European Union, and the European Central Bank,

NOTING that the imbalances of this "euro-area governance" currently confront the European Union with a situation of democratic emergency,

DESIRING to strengthen the democratic accountability and the effectiveness of the institutions of the "governance of the euro area," so that they can better carry out the duties entrusted to them,

RECALLING the Five Presidents' Report, "Completing Europe's Economic and Monetary Union," from June 22, 2015, and its Part V, "Democratic Accountability, Legitimacy and Institutional Strengthening,"

RESOLVED to guarantee the signatory states' repeated commitments toward social rights, as set out in the European Social Charter of October 18, 1961 (revised in 1996), the Community Charter of the Fundamental Social Rights of Workers of December 9, 1989, and the Charter of Fundamental Rights of the European Union, now an integral part of the Lisbon Treaty,

RESOLVED to build the convergence and conditionality policies specific to the euro area around institutions that are democratically accountable at the European and at the national level, in order to fully contribute to achieving the values on which the European integration process is founded,

IN VIEW of further steps to be taken in order to lay the lasting foundation of a political, economic, and social Union,

The Member States of the euro area, signatories of this treaty,

REITERATE their obligation, as Member States of the European Union, to regard their economic policies as a matter of common concern, as well as their responsibility to set up mechanisms ensuring European solidarity;

DECIDE to strengthen the democratic nature of the decisions taken in the framework of the governance of the euro area;

RECALLING the principle of sincere cooperation that governs the relations between the European Union and the Member States,

BEARING IN MIND that the objective of the heads of state or government of the euro-area Member States and of other Member States of the European Union is to incorporate the provisions of this Treaty as soon as possible into the Treaties on which the European Union is founded,

CONSIDERING that the policies of economic and budgetary coordination and fiscal and social convergence necessary for the proper functioning of the euro area relate to the core of the constitutional prerogatives of national Parliaments, which, as recalled by Article 12 TEU, "contribute actively to the good functioning of the Union,"

HAVE AGREED UPON THE FOLLOWING PROVISIONS:

TITLE I. PURPOSE AND SCOPE

ARTICLE 1

1. By this Treaty, the Contracting Parties agree, as Member States of the European Union, to strengthen the policies of economic and budgetary coordination and fiscal and social convergence necessary for the proper functioning of the euro area, by adopting a democratic compact, thereby supporting the achievement of the European Union's objectives.

2. The Contracting Parties are the Member States whose currency is the euro.

As an international treaty uniting the member states of the euro area, the T-Dem stands as a "democratic compact," which offers a counterweight to the European "fiscal compact" concluded in 2013 through the TSCG. To this end, it introduces a Parliamentary Assembly at the heart of the euro-area governance system. An institutional response to the democratic emergency situation Europe currently finds itself in, the T-Dem constitutes a necessary precondition to the reorientation of the economic and budgetary policies currently carried out within the euro area, so that they give greater consideration to fiscal and social convergence.

TITLE II. DEMOCRATIC COMPACT FOR THE EURO AREA

ARTICLE 2. The Parliamentary Assembly

By this Treaty, the Contracting Parties establish among themselves an Assembly called "Parliamentary Assembly of the Euro Area" (hereinafter referred to as "the Assembly").

At the heart of the democratic compact offered by the T-Dem, lies the Parliamentary Assembly of the Euro Area. The Assembly strives to become the institution representing the European peoples within the governance of the euro area. It is composed of both members of national parliaments (who ought to be meaningfully involved in the formulation of the economic, social, and fiscal policies of the euro area) and members of the European Parliament (who represent European citizens), and therefore seeks to enable the participation of citizen representatives to the decision-making processes directly relevant to them.

ARTICLE 3. Functions

1. The Assembly shall, jointly with the Eurogroup, exercise the legislative function and shall assume functions of political control as laid down in this Treaty.

2. The Assembly shall work in close cooperation with the European Parliament.

The Parliamentary Assembly of the Euro Area established by the T-Dem is not meant to supplant any of the European Union institutions, nor is it to question their respective competences.

ARTICLE 4. Composition

1. The number of members of the Assembly shall not exceed 400. It shall be composed, for four-fifths of its members, of representatives designated by national Parliaments in proportion to the groups within them and with due regard to political pluralism, in accordance with a procedure laid down by each euro-area Member State, and for one-fifth of its members, of representatives designated by the European Parliament in proportion to the groups within it and with due regard to political pluralism, in accordance with a procedure laid down by the European Parliament.

2. The number of members of the Assembly designated within national Parliaments shall be fixed in proportion to the population of the euro-area Member States. Each national Parliament sends at least one representative.

3. Delegations from the Parliaments of the Member States of the European Union whose currency is not the euro shall be invited to participate, as observers, in the meetings of the Assembly. They shall have access in due time to all relevant information, and shall be duly consulted.

4. A regulation shall fix the number of members of the Assembly.

The Parliamentary Assembly of the Euro Area is composed of parliament members. Four-fifths of its members are representatives from national parliaments, whereas the remaining one-fifth is composed of representatives from the European Parliament. In that way, the Assembly guarantees the close association of national parliaments to the definition and control of the political choices made intergovernmentally at the euro-area level. As for the involvement of members of the European Parliament, it gives substance to the commitment of "close cooperation" enshrined in Article 3(2). Finally, because it is desirable that both the structures of the euro area and the democratic governance methods set up by the T-Dem evolve over time, it is foreseen that delegations from parliaments of states whose currency is still not the euro may participate, as observers, in the meetings of the Assembly.

The exact composition of each parliamentary delegation (both from national parliaments and the European Parliament) will naturally reflect their own political composition. They will therefore be composed in due proportion to the political groups within them, so that pluralism is guaranteed. Moreover, the T-Dem provides that the size of national delegations will be proportional to the population of the state concerned, on the understanding that each member state shall send at least one representative.

ARTICLE 5. New Members

The other Member States of the European Union can become signatories of this Treaty as from the entry into force of the decision of the Council of the European Union taken in accordance with Article 140(2) TFEU to abrogate their derogation from adopting the euro.

The T-Dem does not set up a closed circle. On the contrary, it is founded on the assumption that a democratic turn in the governance of the euro area and an economic policy shift can restore to the European project the appeal it long ago lost. It therefore keeps the doors open to those who may want to join.

ARTICLE 6. The Council of Ministers of the Euro Area (Eurogroup)

1. The Council of Ministers of the Euro Area shall ensure close coordination and convergence of the economic and fiscal policies of Member States whose currency is the euro.

2. It shall consist, according to the items placed on the agenda, of the Ministers for economic affairs and finance, the Ministers for employment and social affairs, or other Ministers concerned by the agenda.

3. The President of the Council of Ministers of the Euro Area, pursuant to Article 2 to Protocol No. 14 of the Lisbon Treaty, shall be elected by a majority of the Member States.

The Council of Ministers of the Euro Area (Eurogroup) predates the T-Dem. It is an informal advisory body that classically brings together the finance ministers of the euro area. Mentioned in Article 137 and Protocol 14 of the Treaty on the Functioning of the European Union (TFEU), the Eurogroup has emerged as a powerful coordination forum for the various institutions that make up euro-area governance. The T-Dem reasserts the Eurogroup's overall mission (Article 6(1)). However, the T-Dem recalls that economy and finance ministers do not own this Council of Ministers of the Euro Area, which could well alternatively bring together, if the agenda so requires, ministers with other portfolios, starting with employment and social affairs ministers.

TITLE III. POWERS AND TASKS OF THE PARLIAMENTARY ASSEMBLY OF THE EURO AREA

Setting up a Parliamentary Assembly of the Euro Area only makes sense if the Assembly is granted genuine powers. Taking stock of the multifaceted nature of the governance of the euro area, and the diversity of institutions it involves (Euro Summit, Eurogroup, European Commission, Court of Justice of the European Union, European Central Bank), the T-Dem does not seek to reproduce the processes of representative democracy by artificially creating an opposition between a "government" and a "parliament." It instead strives to strengthen the legislative power and to counterbalance the conditionality and convergence policies that this new European executive center has brought about.

ARTICLE 7. Euro Summit and Eurogroup

1. In agreement with the Eurogroup, the Assembly shall prepare the meetings of the Heads of State or Government of the Euro Area (Euro Summits).

2. In agreement with its members, it shall determine the semiannual work program of the Eurogroup.

The Euro Summit is the highest decision-making body within the governance of the euro area. It brings together the heads of state and government of member states whose currency is the euro, and the president of the European Commission. Currently outside the Treaty framework, it defines the strategic orientations for the conduct of economic policies, the improvement of competitiveness, and the strengthening of convergence. Currently, another executive institution, the Eurogroup (the Council of Ministers of the Euro Area, see Art. 6), controls the organization of these Summits, which are to take place twice a year: the Eurogroup is in charge of the preparation of and the follow-up to the Summit meetings; it moreover plays a decisive role as an agenda-setter. Article 7(1) of the T-Dem provides for, and organizes, the involvement of the Parliamentary Assembly of the Euro Area in this secretive platform, which currently is dominated by national and European executives. It authorizes the Assembly to participate to the preparation of the Euro Summit meetings, and therefore strengthens the Assembly's role in defining the policies carried out in the euro area. On this specific point, and in light of solutions inspired from a critical analysis of concrete practices, Article 7(1) provides that the president of the Euro Summit shall submit the draft agenda to the Assembly, which may then, in agreement with the Eurogroup, add items. The Assembly is thus endowed with the means of meaningfully weighing in on the agenda of the Euro Summit, and influencing the choices it makes.

ARTICLE 8. Convergence and Coordination of Economic and Budgetary Policies

1. Each year, the Assembly shall adopt a position on the *Alert Mechanism Report* (AMR) released by the European Commission in the framework of the macroeconomic imbalance procedure, as far as it relates to Member States whose currency is the euro.

The "European Semester" process has developed an alert mechanism that aims at facilitating the early detection and follow-up of serious macroeconomic imbalance within a member state, most notably when they risk jeopardizing the proper functioning of the Economic and Monetary Union. The Commission prepares a report known as the Alert Mechanism Report, which is later examined by the Eurogroup. The Eurogroup independently decides if a member state is or is not affected by an excessive imbalance. Article 8(1) involves the Parliamentary Assembly of the Euro Area in the examination of this report. The Assembly participates in the determination of excessive imbalances, and the definition of country-specific recommendations addressed to affected member states.

2. The Assembly shall take part in the monitoring of the discussions on the annual draft budgetary plans of the Member States in the framework of the European Semester and shall make recommendations.

In the framework of the European Semester process, member states submit "national reform programs for growth and jobs" and "stability programs," in which they outline their policy plans with regard to structural reforms and fiscal discipline. On that basis, the Eurogroup addresses guidelines to the member states with regard to their economic and employment policies, and their budgetary trajectories. These guidelines are to be duly taken into account by national authorities when designing their budgets. Again, the Eurogroup is not politically accountable for its interventions, despite the fact that it directly influences national budgetary policies.

Article 8(2) addresses this democratic gap by involving the Assembly in the assessment of the draft budgetary plans submitted by the member states. Moreover, the Assembly is entitled to issue its own recommendations on the economic and employment policies, and the budgetary trajectory of the member states, that they are to take into account.

3. As the case may be, the Assembly shall assess the recommendations and reports submitted by the European Commission to the Council concerning the euro-area Member States subject to an excessive imbalance procedure.

Every member state subject to an excessive imbalance procedure is to submit a "corrective action plan" to the Eurogroup and the Commission. The Eurogroup, on the basis of a Commission report, assesses the plan within two months of its submission.

Article 8(3) states that the Assembly is to express its views on the substance of this plan. If it deems it appropriate, it endorses the plan and participates in the definition of the list of specific actions necessary to correct the imbalance. But it is also entitled to amend it, and to challenge the prescriptions of the Eurogroup, which is to take the Assembly's observations into account.

4. The Assembly shall hold regular exchanges of views on the implementation conditions of the structural reforms recommended for the euro area within the framework of the European Semester.

5. The Assembly shall take part in the supervision of the euro-area Member States' coordination efforts in the field of budgetary policies, and shall monitor the overall fiscal trajectory of the euro area.

ARTICLE 9. Financial Assistance Facility

1. In the framework of the procedure for granting stability support, the Parliamentary Assembly of the Euro Area shall approve by a vote the financial assistance facility granted under the procedure referred to in Article 13(2) of the Treaty Establishing the European Stability Mechanism.

2. If the financial assistance facility as referred to in paragraph 1 is approved by the Assembly, the memorandum of understanding detailing the conditionality attached to the financial assistance facility shall be submitted to the Assembly for approval.

3. The Assembly shall take part in the assessment of the situation of the Member States benefiting from or having benefited from a macroeconomic adjustment program.

Article 13 of the Treaty Establishing the European Stability Mechanism (ESM) organizes the procedure through which financial assistance can be granted to a euro-area member state in order to preserve its financial stability. The ESM is thus an emergency fund. It is run by the

Board of Governors, bringing together the finance ministers of euro-area member states. In other words, these are again the members of the Eurogroup, wearing a different hat, sitting around the table. Moreover, the Board of Governors is chaired by the president of the Eurogroup.

The Eurogroup manages all aspects of the ESM's activities: it approves the decisions to grant financial assistance to a euro-area member state; it determines the conditions under which the assistance is to be granted; and most importantly, it concludes the memorandums of understanding detailing the conditionality attached to ESM financial assistance. Greece, Ireland, Spain, and Portugal have already "benefited" from such assistance, against drastic reform commitments in the field of budgetary policy. The most paradigmatic example is, of course, Greece. Four main conditions were featured in the Memorandum of Understanding signed by Greece in August 2015: a primary surplus of 3.5% GDP, fiscal reforms involving a deep overhaul of the VAT and the pension systems, far-reaching budgetary cuts in the public sector, a substantial labor market reform, and a large privatization program.

The T-Dem seeks here to subject a particularly untransparent decision-making process to the possibility of political control: the positive vote of the Parliamentary Assembly of the Euro Area will now be necessary to grant financial assistance to a state, and each memorandum of understanding negotiated by the Eurogroup will have to obtain the Assembly's approval.

ARTICLE 10. Governance Dialogue with the European Central Bank

1. Each year, in the light of the economic forecasts, the Assembly shall be invited to adopt a position through a resolution on the interpretation of the price stability objective and the inflation target adopted by the European Central Bank, in compliance with the Treaties on which the European Union is founded.

2. The Assembly shall approve by vote the annual report of the European Central Bank on the Single Supervisory Mechanism.

Endowed with an unprecedented level of independence, the European Central Bank remains, to many, at the margins of the European public space. However, with the eurozone crisis, the Frankfurt institution has experienced a substantial expansion of its prerogatives. In 2012 Mario Draghi even portrayed himself as the last guardian of the monetary union, famously pledging that the ECB would do "whatever it takes" to save the euro. The T-Dem puts an end to this splendid isolation, and creates the institutional environment for a continuous public debate on the economic and monetary choices of the ECB.

ARTICLE 11. Powers of Investigation and Control

1. In order to carry out its function of control of the institutions of the "governance of the euro area," and in close cooperation with the European Parliament, the Assembly of the Euro Area is endowed with a Parliamentary Office for the Evaluation of European Economic Choices.

2. The Assembly may, at the request of a quarter of its members, set up a committee of inquiry responsible for investigating alleged maladministration in the "euro-area governance."

3. The European Court of Auditors shall assist the Assembly in exercising its control functions.

4. The European Central Bank and the European Commission shall supply to the Assembly all documents and data which the latter considers desirable in the exercise of its powers. As the case may be, these documents and data may be examined by a parliamentary committee that will meet on camera.

5. In order to ensure transparency and accountability, the Assembly may hear institutional actors of the euro-area governance.

Exercising political oversight over the governance of the euro area is certainly no easy task. It is not only the technical sophistication of the issues at stake that is problematic—even though it certainly discourages

the many representatives who are not familiar with the complex economic and legal reasoning that discussing euro-area governance requires. Also problematic is the deep information asymmetry between
the economic and financial institutions, either national or European,
and the members of parliaments. The latter frequently deliberate on
the basis of economic assessments and statistical data produced elsewhere, which deprives them of the intellectual independence they require in order to exercise meaningful political oversight. Worse still,
willful representatives are often faced with major opposition from
these institutions, which, like the European Central Bank, are keen to
preserve their "trade secrets" and resist the transparency requirements
necessary to a genuine democratic debate.

The T-Dem intends to endow the Parliamentary Assembly of the Euro
Area with the necessary means to exercise political oversight. It establishes a Parliamentary Office for the Evaluation of European Economic
Choices, tasked with producing autonomous data on euro-area governance. It entitles the Assembly to gain access to all documents and data
owned by the other key institutions of the euro area. This will enable the
Assemble to become a central forum where a truly transnational public
debate on European economic choices will develop.

ARTICLE 12. Exercise of Legislative Competence within the Euro Area

1. Without undermining the competences conferred upon the Union in
the field of economic policy, the Assembly and the Eurogroup, acting in
accordance with the legislative procedures referred to in Articles 13 and
15, shall adopt legal provisions to foster sustainable growth and employment within the euro area, social cohesion, and better convergence of
economic and fiscal policies.

2. The Assembly and the Eurogroup, acting in accordance with the ordinary legislative procedure, shall vote on the base and the rate of the
corporate tax that contributes to the euro-area budget.

3. In compliance with the corporate tax base fixed at Article 12(2),
Member States may adopt an additional tax rate.

4. The Assembly and the Eurogroup, acting in accordance with the ordinary legislative procedure, shall adopt the provisions with a view to pool public debts exceeding 60% of each euro-area Member State's GDP.

5. The legislative act projects or legislative act proposals provided for in Article 13 shall first be sent to the European Parliament for an opinion.

In order to guarantee the ability of the Parliamentary Assembly of the Euro Area to positively weigh in on the orientation of economic policies within the euro area, the T-Dem endows the Assembly with a general legislative competence with regard to sustainable growth, employment, social cohesion, and convergence of economic and fiscal policies. Such competence lies in the field of "shared competences" between the European Union and the member states, meaning concretely that states retain the competence for themselves as long as the Union has not legislated. Supplementing the European Union, the Assembly would thus exercise its legislative prerogatives "without undermining the competences conferred upon the Union." The legislative basis of Article 12 also jointly tasks the Assembly and the Eurogroup to vote on the base and the rate of the corporate tax that contributes to the euro-area budget, and to pool public debts exceeding 60% of each euro-area member state's GDP.

ARTICLE 13. Ordinary Legislative Procedure

1. The Eurogroup and the Assembly shall jointly adopt the legislative acts applicable within the euro-area governance.

2. Legislative initiative concurrently belongs to the members of the Eurogroup and to the members of the Assembly. They have a right of amendment.

3. The legislative agenda of the euro area shall be set jointly by the Eurogroup and the Assembly. However, within the limit of half of the meetings, the Assembly shall set as a priority its own agenda and place the legislative act projects or proposals it accepts.

4. The ordinary legislative procedure of the euro area applies to the regulations, directives, and decisions jointly adopted by the Eurogroup and the Assembly.

5. The members of the Eurogroup submit legislative act projects. The members of the Assembly submit legislative act proposals.

6. Every legislative act project or proposal shall be successively examined by the Eurogroup and the Assembly in view of the adoption of a single text.

7. When, following disagreement between the two institutions, a legislative act project or proposal could not be adopted after two readings, the President of the Eurogroup and the President of the Assembly shall within six weeks convene a meeting of the Conciliation Committee.

8. The Conciliation Committee, which shall be composed of the members of the Eurogroup or their representatives and an equal number of members representing the Assembly, shall have the task of reaching an agreement on a joint text for the provisions still under discussion, within six weeks of its being convened.

9. If, within that six-week period, the Conciliation Committee approves a joint text, the Assembly and the Eurogroup shall each have a period of six weeks from that approval in which to adopt the act in question in accordance with the joint text.

10. If within the six weeks of its being convened the Conciliation Committee does not approve a joint text, or if the text mentioned in paragraph 9 is not adopted, the President of the Eurogroup, after a new reading within both the Eurogroup and the Assembly, requests that the Assembly takes a final decision.

Article 13 provides an ordinary legislative procedure to implement the policies foreseen by Article 12. It states that legislative initiative belongs to both the members of the Assembly and those of the Eurogroup, who also have a right of amendment. That is major aspect of the T-Dem: it is well known that the European Parliament is deprived of legislative initiative and prevented from effectively weigh on the Union's agenda, thereby substantially weakening the democratic credentials of the European political system. In this case, on the contrary, the Assembly dominates each aspect of the legislative procedure, and is therefore in a position to democratically set the pace of the euro area's consolidation.

The T-Dem foresees that legislative acts will be jointly adopted by the Assembly and the Eurogroup. The procedure seeks to foster the emergence of compromises between the two institutions, but the last word is left to the Assembly, which is therefore endowed with a powerful instrument to influence the policies conducted within the euro area.

Agenda-setting crucially conditions the balance of an institutional system, most particularly when it comes to the relationship between the executive and legislative branches. Holding the right to legislative initiative is often not sufficient for the latter, as it must also be in a position to effectively use it. Article 13(3) shows that the T-Dem takes this potential pitfall seriously. In order to avoid creating a system that overwhelmingly advantages the executive, which is often better equipped to draft legislative proposals, a safeguard was introduced in order to guarantee that, in case of tension, the Assembly retains control over half of the agenda, whatever the power relationship between the two institutions.

ARTICLE 14. Budget of the Euro Area

1. The budget of the euro area shall aim at fostering sustainable growth, employment, social cohesion, and better convergence of economic and fiscal policies within the euro area.

2. All items of revenue and expenditure of the euro area shall be included in estimates to be drawn up for each financial year and shall be shown in the budget.

3. The annual budget of the euro area shall be established by the Assembly and the Eurogroup.

4. The financial year runs from January 1 to December 31.

ARTICLE 15. Legislative Procedure Applicable to the Adoption of the Budget of the Euro Area

1. The Assembly and the Eurogroup establish the budget of the euro area in accordance with the following provisions.

2. On the basis of a budget proposal prepared by the Assembly, the Eurogroup adopts a budget project.

3. The budget proposal and the budget project shall contain an estimate of revenue and an estimate of expenditure.

4. The Eurogroup shall submit its budget project to the Assembly not later than September 1 of the year preceding that in which the budget is to be implemented. If within 40 days of such submission, the Parliamentary Assembly of the Euro area:

(a) approves the budget project, the budget shall be adopted.
(b) has not taken a decision, a new budget project shall be submitted by the Eurogroup.
(c) adopts amendments by a majority of its component members, the amended project shall be forwarded to the Eurogroup. The President of the Assembly, in agreement with the President of the Eurogroup, shall immediately convene a meeting of the Conciliation Committee. However, if within 10 days of the project being forwarded, the Eurogroup informs the Assembly that it has approved all its amendments, the Conciliation Committee shall not meet.

5. The Conciliation Committee, which shall be composed of the members of the Eurogroup or their representatives and an equal number of members of the Assembly, shall have the task of reaching agreement on a joint text, on the basis of the positions of the Assembly and the Eurogroup.

6. (a) If, within 21 days, the Conciliation Committee agrees on a joint text, the Assembly and the Eurogroup shall each have a period of 14 days from the date of that agreement to approve the joint text.

(b) If, within the 21 days referred to in subparagraph 6(a), the Conciliation Committee does not agree on a joint text, a new budget project shall be submitted by the Eurogroup.

7. If, within the period of 14 days referred to in subparagraph 6(a):

(a) the Assembly and the Eurogroup approve the joint text, the budget shall be deemed to be definitively adopted.
(b) the Assembly rejects the joint text by a majority of its component members, a new budget project shall be submitted by the Eurogroup, taking account of the positions of the Assembly.
(c) the Eurogroup rejects the joint text, the President of the Eurogroup shall request the Assembly, acting by a majority of its component Members, to take a final decision.

Article 15 sets up a special legislative procedure for the adoption of the budget. The general idea is that the Assembly and the Eurogroup jointly adopt the budget.

However, the procedure put forward by the T-Dem has its own specificities. The preparation of budgetary laws is a complex, technical task with which parliamentary assemblies tend to be less comfortable than executives, most notably in view of the expertise required to draft them. This element has contributed to progressively reduce the influence exerted by assemblies on budgetary and economic choices in modern democracies, despite the fact that voting the budget historically constituted their main raison d'être. The T-Dem thus provides that the first budgetary guidelines, which are to initiate the procedure, shall be elaborated by the Assembly. In other words, this first draft will set the frame, and allow the Assembly to push its own priorities. It is on the basis of this first draft that the Eurogroup will adopt a project for the euro-area budget.

The final adoption of this budgetary project will require that the project be approved, in identical terms, by both institutions. Again, the procedure seeks to foster the emergence of compromises between the Assembly and the Eurogroup, while leaving the final say to the Assembly.

ARTICLE 16. The Euro Area's Own Resources

1. The euro area shall provide itself with the means necessary to attain its objectives and carry through its policies.

2. Without prejudice to other revenue, the budget shall be financed wholly from the euro area's own resources.

3. The euro area's own resources shall be those set out in Article 12.

ARTICLE 17. Appointments

After hearing them, the Assembly shall vote on the candidates chosen for the Executive Board of the European Central Bank, the Presidency of the Eurogroup, and the Managing Direction of the European Stability Mechanism.

As a last testimony of its actual power, the Parliamentary Assembly of the Euro Area is associated to the appointments within the main institutions of the euro area: the executive board of the European Central Bank, the presidency of the Council of Ministers of the euro area (Eurogroup), and the managing direction of the ESM. The Assembly hears the candidates for these positions, and votes on each one of them.

TITLE IV. CONSISTENCY AND RELATIONSHIP WITH THE LAW OF THE UNION

ARTICLE 18

This Treaty shall be applied and interpreted by the Contracting Parties in conformity with the Treaties on which the European Union is founded, in particular Article 4(3) of the Treaty on European Union, and with European Union law, including procedural law whenever the adoption of secondary legislation is required.

The T-Dem does not derogate or question the law of the European Union. Its objective is an entirely different one: it democratizes the governance of the euro area. Mindful not to hinder the European project, it is meant to be applied and interpreted in accordance with the principle of sincere cooperation that binds all institutional actors of the Union.

TITLE V. GENERAL AND FINAL PROVISIONS

ARTICLE 19

This Treaty shall be ratified by the Contracting Parties in accordance with their respective constitutional requirements.

ARTICLE 20

This Treaty shall enter into force on . . . 2019, provided that half of the Member States whose currency is the euro on the day of signature of this Treaty, and representing 70% of their population, have deposited their instruments of ratification, or at any prior date on which these conditions would be met.

Even if a joint ratification by all nineteen euro-area member states would be ideal, it is crucial to ensure a swift entry into force of the T-Dem, in order to accelerate the necessary emergence of a democratic counterweight within the euro area. With the representation of European peoples at the core of its raison d'être, the T-Dem includes a classic clause providing that its entry into force will be triggered by its ratification by a certain number of signatory states (in this case, half of the euro-area member states—that is, ten of them), representing at least 70% of the population of those states.

ARTICLE 21

This Treaty shall apply as from the date of entry into force among the Contracting Parties whose currency is the euro that have ratified it.

ARTICLE 22

Within five years, at most, of the date of entry into force of this Treaty, on the basis of an assessment of the experience with its implementation, the necessary steps shall be taken, in accordance with the Treaty on European Union and the Treaty on the Functioning of the European Union, with the aim of incorporating the substance of this Treaty into the legal framework of the European Union.

Done at Brussels, on . . . 2019, in a single original, whose Dutch, English, Estonian, Finnish, French, German, Greek, Irish, Italian, Latvian, Lithuanian, Maltese, Portuguese, Slovak, Slovenian, and Spanish texts are equally authentic, which shall be deposited in the archives of the Depositary, which shall transmit a duly certified copy to each of the Contracting Parties,

For the euro-area Member States.

—Translated by Paul Dermine

PART THREE

DEBATE NOW!

7

Europe's Constituent Moment

JEREMY ADELMAN AND ANNE-LAURE DELATTE

The Old World is in trouble. But it also faces a historic opportunity, a constituent moment. A constituent moment is one in which political subjects claim the ability and authority to co-govern a shared world, a world in which they become a people through the exercise of voice and political representation. A constituent moment is one that resets the democratic legitimacy of the polity. This is what the Old World needs, to get out of trouble.[1]

A prolonged economic slump, a debt crisis it can't shake, and malaise in the face of the humanitarian catastrophe generated by waves of asylum seekers from the Middle East and North Africa have revealed the depleted state of European institutions. Europeans are more interdependent than ever; but their system of government is unable to cope with the pileup of challenges and crises. This erodes confidence in the institutions that braced Europe together for the past six decades.

Frailty in Europe means a weak link in the wider interdependent world. As the world's largest economy, Europe is an engine of global wealth. It is a major front in the fight against terror. It is the main hope for terror's first victims—the refugees. With prosperity, security, and humanity at stake, a weak Europe weakens everyone else. For this reason, it is in the world's interest to understand how integration went awry—and how to get it back on track. *How to Democratize Europe* charts a compelling way to an alternative future.

The End of the European Miracle

For the past six decades, the continent has followed a model of integration that brought it peace, affluence, and social betterment. That model was premised on political compromises involving multiple governments with heterogeneous preferences. Intergovernmental bargaining and divergent preferences led to lowest-common-denominator solutions.[2]

Under these conditions, the model of integration worked remarkably well. After 1945, a coterie of European leaders agreed that a lasting peace required more than the simple coexistence of rivalrous countries on the crowded fringe of Eurasia. Coexistence had been the mainstay of European diplomacy since the Congress of Vienna in 1815; it broke down in 1914; it imploded in 1939. Instead, these new federalists argued, European states needed to embrace their interdependence and bury old enmities. What followed was the systematic dismantling, step by step, of national sovereignty on the continent.

The process started with the alignment of France and Germany under the Schuman Plan in 1950, which put their coal and steel production under a common, binational roof. The Netherlands, Belgium, Italy, and Luxembourg soon followed, forming a core of relatively homogeneous democratic welfare states, built upon industrial societies that shared a common identity and common values, all sharing pooled resources.

But this foundation has grown increasingly shaky since the Union's early days. It was premised on a common memory of a horrid war. Bargaining worked well as long as the world economy was growing rapidly. Those conditions are now gone.

First, the initial tightly-knotted Union eventually sprawled, spreading southward and eastward, incorporating states like Spain and Greece. (Even the standoffish Brits joined in 1973, though they did not embrace the common currency.) This spread diluted the homogeneity of the original club—but the Union held, thanks in part to the Cold War, which created a common foe and allowed Western leaders to hold up the Union of democratic, capitalist European societies as a counterpoint to the centrally planned regimes.

Second, the fall of the Berlin Wall removed the threat from the Soviet Union. With no common enemy and no common identity, what remained to hold Europe together? All that was left was the economy, which, for a time, looked like a powerful binding force. Indeed, the sprawl eastward to Poland and other former Warsaw Bloc countries was part of a general effort to support market-friendly transitions from planned economies. European integration was seen fundamentally *as* economic, as if political institutions existed merely to serve the market.

Third, the old heavy-metal economy of reindustrializing Europe gave way to a new model. The original coal-and-steel coalition has yielded to a nimbler moneyed market, transforming the Union from a trading bloc to a dynamic financial bloc. Today, capital crisscrosses European borders in sums and velocities that eclipse the older flows of commodities. The introduction of a common currency only sped up this transformation: In the wake of the euro rollout in January 1999, the financial imbalances between lending countries and borrowing countries billowed.

The New Old World

The past decade has exposed Europe's fundamental weaknesses, starting with its economic defects. The massive capital flows across the continent weren't a problem as long as the money kept moving from richer countries to poorer ones, from savers to spenders, from the old core to the newer peripheral members. But capital flows reversed in 2010 in the wake of the Wall Street meltdown: after a decade of infusion, households, banks, and firms in borrowing countries saw money stampeding out, leaving them unable to service their debts.

The structures of the Union snapped under the weight of the crisis. The priorities of the two founding countries did not align: Today, Germany is a creditor and France a debtor, and they diverge on how to manage the string of financial crises that have affected Europe since 2008. Thus, instead of a coordinated and collaborative response, leaders resorted to emergency last-minute solutions that only just succeeded in preventing catastrophe but set off a ruinous spiral of public sector borrowing. Budget deficits ballooned, putting governments at the mercy of their creditors. The effect was to partition Europe into two blocs locked in a winner-take-all struggle. Gone was any sense of shared interest, not to mention higher purpose: Creditor countries came together to impose conditions on debtors; Greece and other borrowers withdrew, after a ruckus, into a kind of sullen silence. In a horrible, perverse trap, governments have had to muzzle the discontents of their citizens lest unrest spur more capital flight and more misery. All that is left on the horizon is endless austerity, deteriorating faith in public institutions, and a Europe more divided than any time since the fall of the Berlin Wall.

Then Europe got thumped by the migrant crisis—which perhaps even more than the financial crisis has brought into sharp relief the Union's incapacity for decision making. Unrest in the Middle East and parts of Africa has sent more than a million asylum seekers across the Mediterranean, about half of them from Syria. Attempts to share the humanitarian burden have pulled back the veil on the depth of Europe's various divides. Unable to act in concert, the current governance has pushed crisis management down to the national level. Countries like Germany and Sweden have thrown open their doors, to the dismay of many of their neighbors; Poland and Hungary have refused to take in asylum seekers. Fences went up all over the Balkans. One of the pillars of European integration—the Schengen system, which created open borders for the internal movement of people—is on life support. The spate of terror attacks has only emboldened the skeptics' view of European authorities as incapable of doing the bare minimum expected of states: keep citizens safe.

Europe suffers from the global ennui with ruling classes. This is especially dangerous to the fabric of the Union because it relied so heavily on intergovernmental, elite-to-elite bargaining. The populist rebellion against government by closely knit insiders, who govern by consensus-building and share the same underlying ideologies and values, has emboldened a new generation of nativists who thrive off blaming plutocrats in Brussels for their countries' woes.

The old Franco-German bond was based upon intergovernmental agreements between ruling circles who were willing to share sovereignty—but not necessarily to open up decision making to democratic principles and practices. The original founders formed a cliquey, visionary group who promised the public greater opportunities for consumption and personal betterment but kept the reins of public power for themselves. The result was a Union with some technocratic prowess but weak democratic foundations.

Constituent Moment

Europe badly needs a reset. It could go back to another round of bargaining. But each new deal enjoys less legitimacy than the old one that had ceased to work. Hunkering down on a failing strategy, especially given the scale of the migrant, security, economic, and ecological challenges, is likely to lead to less agreement, less legitimacy, and greater room for exiteers.

The source of the problem is political. The representative institutions no longer work; they were never meant to be robust anyway, never meant to serve as a way for Europeans to self-identify and deliberate as a European people. They do not accommodate the diversity of Europe into a functioning democratic polyarchy—a regime that accommodates a diversity of interests and lets constituents that feel that their claims are honored, which breeds loyalty, or are effectively voiced, which breeds legitimacy. Faced with waves of crises, officials retreated into their bunkers. Emergency management eclipsed already-anemic democratic decision making. And when that failed—as it often did—national leaders, in order to prevent disasters, found themselves corralled into hastily arranged summits, which have done little to bolster confidence in the underlying structures.

There is a fix. It rests on moving decision making from a depleted bargaining model to a new, invigorating, deliberative model. And this requires the creation of a system of active representation and public debate so that decisions are understood, recognized, and legitimate.

It also rests on rejecting principles of integration that have performed as if European Union comes at the expense of national sovereignty, as if what's good for Europe is less good for the Netherlands or Italy, as if it's Europe *or* the nation-state. Old federalists and new isolationists agree on one thing: Both see "integration" as an either-or solution—either leaders surrender national sovereignty to supranational authorities or they defend the homeland. Those who hope to keep the Union together need to find a way out of that deadlock—because right now, it is very hard to make a compelling case for deepening a Union that does not promise anything more than austerity, more dysfunction, and less control. National leaders are more hesitant than ever to transfer power to a distant European Parliament, at the very time when we need coordinated, representative decision making to make Europe functional again.

A constituent moment presents the opportunity for a new founding—the start of a second era for a modern, peaceable Europe. Instead of resting on the original founding practices of technocratic bargaining, the new founding needs to resolve the legitimacy gap in public institutions. Instead of deal making, this book outlines a model of representation in which the popular enactment of rights to have a say in the rules governing Europeans' future can rely on institutions that mobilize, channel, and articulate those rights. This book offers a way to rebalance bureaucratic authority, regulation, and enforcement with democratic debate, contention, and agreement.

To take a metaphor from economics, one might say that this book offers a way to shift from a Europe made by political "taking" to one of political "making," from accepting expedient deals to creating legitimate agreement.

This book outlines a premise for the Union that transcends the either-or logic of integration or sovereignty. It explains how decision-making capacity can grow without simply relocating power from democratic nation states to a less-democratic supranational state. It charts a way to burnish the democratic and deliberative credentials of European lawmakers.

Notes

1. Jason Frank, *Constituent Moments: Enacting the People in Postrevolutionary America* (Durham, NC: Duke University Press, 2010).
2. Andrew Moravcsik, *The Choice for Europe: Social Purpose and State Power from Messina to Maastricht* (Ithaca, NY: Cornell University Press, 1998).

8

Ten Thoughts on the Treaty Democratizing the Euro Area (T-Dem)

PAUL MAGNETTE

1. The diagnosis made by the authors of the T-Dem is clear and sound. The divorce between the European Union and its citizens originates in the seizure, in the full sense of the term, of decision-making powers by a handful of national and European governments and officials. Repositioning elected representatives—from the national, regional, and European level—at the heart of the governance process is the only consistent answer to that issue. Whereas the Treaty of the European Union itself states in its Article 15 that the European Council "shall not exercise legislative functions," the genesis of the TSCG or fiscal compact is a blatant violation of the letter and the spirit of the EU's "constitution," a "legal coup" even, which demands a genuine democratic remedy.

2. From a formal perspective, in a Union where socioeconomic competences are widely shared between the European and national (if not subnational) levels, democratic responsibilities should also be shared between these various power levels. European representatives lack the presence in national public spaces to legitimately claim exclusive representation of the citizenry. It is thus essential to associate national representatives in the setting of the Union's priorities, following a logic of "transnational socialization" of European matters.

3. The adoption of a "reform treaty" currently represents the only possible path, as a comprehensive overhaul of the treaties seems unrealistic in the short or medium term, and given the limits that the scenario of a federalist leap highlighted in the 2003–2004 Constitutional Convention experience. As a consequence, drawing inspiration from the TSCG method, while altering its terms, looks like the best tactical approach. From this perspective, the provisions on the entry into force and consolidation of the T-Dem (Articles 20 to 22) are particularly well thought out.

4. The objective of such a radical reform is to strengthen the socio-economic cohesion of the euro area, through partial debt mutualization and by providing the zone with the budgetary, fiscal, and social foundations it lacks. This objective, which, as shown by T-Dem's recitals, are perfectly in line with the fundamental principles of European integration, is likely to be endorsed by federalists. It should lay the basis for a new European social contract, and lead the member states that do not share such endeavors to renegotiate their relationship with the EU. The current Treaty structure, which enables some member states to remain outside the euro area, while benefiting from all the other advantages of Union membership, is not sustainable in the long term, as it can only exacerbate the asymmetries and tensions between a deeply integrated euro area and the rest of the EU. From this perspective, Brexit serves as an opportunity for a fundamental rethink.

5. An Assembly composed of national and European representatives would serve as a necessary democratic counterweight to the European Council and its underlying network of bureaucracies and diplomatic services. Moreover, this innovation would be likely to build bridges between the supporters of a Union that's more deeply rooted within its sociopolitical territories and federalists championing the idea of European economic and fiscal government.

6. The composition of such an Assembly must rely on the principle of parliamentary representation. The Council of Ministers may well represent the member states in the same way the German Bundesrat does for the *Länder*, but it does not sufficiently reflect the diversity of European public opinion. The weights to assign to the different European parliaments is a delicate issue, consid-

ering the substantial differences of size among the member states (art. 4 T-Dem). The national delegations of federal states could include both national and regional representatives, without altering the democratic logic of the envisaged model. As for the European Parliament—if, as we assume below, the respective roles and prerogatives of both Assemblies are better defined, it should not necessarily be represented in the new Assembly.

7. The creation of such an Assembly is fully justified by the deep inadequacy of the role entrusted to national parliaments by the Treaties and the relevant Protocol. Following a defensive logic, national parliaments could be given, in the framework of the EMU, control powers equivalent to those they enjoy under the Area of Freedom, Security and Justice (art. 69 TFEU) or in the field of judicial cooperation in civil matters (art. 81 TFEU). Because the coordination of budgetary, economic, and social policies affects essential competences of member states and their regions (in the same way that mixed commercial agreements do), national and regional parliaments should at the very least be granted an effective power to monitor and control compliance with the subsidiarity and proportionality principles (as some parliaments indeed already do), and perhaps even to reject legislative acts that intrude upon sensitive national issues, such as social protection or the organization of public services.

8. Beyond this "negative" power, the Assembly must also be able to act positively and contribute to the decision-making process in the socioeconomic field. I am, however, of the opinion that the legislative function ought to be more neatly distinguished from that of political control, in order to avoid adding further complexities to the European institutional system, and to avoid pointless competition between the European Parliament and the new Assembly. It is already partly the case with the T-Dem, which endows its Assembly with a controlling power over the alert mechanism, draft budgetary plans, Commission recommendations, structural efforts, and coordination of national policies (art. 8 T-Dem), dialogue with the ECB (art. 9 T-Dem), and the appointment of the ECB, Eurogroup, and ESM presidents (art. 17 T-Dem). The tools for political control that are granted to the Assembly (art. 11 T-Dem) also follow that logic.

9. The main difficulty lies in the exercise of the legislative function. To effectively carry out its legislative mission, the new Assembly must be associated in the definition of the agenda of the European Council and the Eurogroup (as foreseen by art. 7 T-Dem), it must vote on and supervise the application of the financial assistance facilities (as provided by art. 9 T-Dem), and it is essential that the composition of the Council of Ministers reflects the items placed on its agenda (art. 6 T-Dem), so that the voices of the ministers for social affairs and employment are not systematically marginalized by those of the finance ministers. In contrast, the respective powers of the European Parliament and the new Assembly under Articles 12 to 14 should be better delineated. Within a Union endowed with true budgetary, economic, and fiscal powers, it is all but nonsensical that the budget and economic and fiscal legislative acts are voted on by the European Parliament. Otherwise, and as long as some EU member states remain outside the euro area, there is a high risk that contradictions emerge between the budgets and legislation of the euro area and those of the rest of the Union. It would therefore be more logical for the European Parliament to vote on the budget and the common fiscal bases, whereas the new Assembly would focus on the democratization of socioeconomic policies falling under the shared competences of the Union (social policy, employment, and so forth). If the new Assembly's *raison d'être* is to overcome power seizure by the European Council, it is by reference to the role of the latter, and not that of the Eurogroup, that the functions of the Assembly ought to be defined. At the earlier stages, its role should consist in defining the legislative agenda, and at the latter, in controlling the European Commission in its role as guardian of the treaties. The Assembly would meet four times a year and have the Commission submit for debate its legislative proposals, its draft Broad Economic Policy Guidelines (art. 121 TFEU), and the acts it takes in the framework of the excessive deficit procedure (art. 126 TFEU), employment policies coordination (art. 148 TFEU), and any other relevant field of shared competence (social policy, healthcare, industry, cohesion, and such). The Assembly could also be endowed with an indirect power of legislative initiative in all these fields, similar to that the European Parliament already enjoys.

10. Other initiatives for further democratizing the Union should not be neglected. The introduction of a real European Social Dialogue is still necessary, as political democracy remains intrinsically linked to social democracy in a majority of member states. The Citizen's Initiative (art. 11 TEU) has a great potential for mobilizing civil society and acting as a counterpower to the Commission's action and failures to act, and the Assembly could certainly give it more resonance, through its legislative initiative power. Moreover, it remains desirable, in view of furthering "transnational socialization" of European issues, to strengthen the Commission's politicization. The new Assembly could also be given a role, complementary to that of the European Parliament, in the appointment and eventual dismissal of the European Commission, as it exists in some federal systems (hearings, inquiries, impeachment, and so on).

– 9 –

For a Demoicratization
of Eurozone Governance

KALYPSO NICOLAIDIS

The governance of the eurozone touches people's lives in more profound ways than the EU has ever done before. This is why citizens
and their politics must own its decisions. Indeed, the essence of the EU
is that the countries that compose it are both states and member states,
whose governments bear the dual responsibility of steering their economies autonomously at home and together in Brussels. The T-Dem, the
proposal for democratizing the governance of the euro area, is an important and valid attempt to bring eurozone governance closer to this dual
reality. Let us create a Parliamentary Assembly as the legislative branch
of European Monetary Union (EMU) governance, its proponents argue;
let this Assembly be composed of national and European parliamentarians; and let's give this Assembly significant powers of oversight over
governance of the Economic and Monetary Union (EMU).

Legitimacy matters because, in the end, the sustainability of all
human institutions is grounded in the ideas that the people whose interests they are supposed to serve hold in their minds. If enough people
stop believing in an institution—like the state or marriage or money—
it will eventually wither away, at least without coercion.

What makes an institution legitimate? Let's simplify. Of the three
core sources of legitimacy—purposive, performative, and procedural—
the first two have been found wanting in the EU. The first was certainly

the secret of its initial success, with the purpose of the EU defined as a mission for eternal peace and ever-rising prosperity, a mission that was entrusted to a chosen few, the techno-managers of the Union's machinery. This approach has run its course, not because the EU has lost its *raison d'être*—it has not—but because the messianic logic that allowed its leaders to overlook the wising-up of the crowds has run its course. No longer can governments argue through the mouthpiece of EU institutions that the end justifies the means because Brussels or EU law or European interests say so.

The second source of legitimacy—performance, or results—will be effective in shoring up an institution in good times, but is by definition a fair-weather resource. When shocks generated endogenously or exogenously hit the polity—and they always will—the polity suffers. In a polity where you cannot "throw the rascals out," the risk is that the people will turn to the next best thing—to throw the whole lot out.

If you cannot completely rely either on purpose or on performance, you must turn to process. Process grants legitimacy simply when, whatever the aim or quality of the decision taken, it is owned, and owned by those affected by it. Writ large, this is the logic of democracy as the ultimate source of legitimacy.

There has been much debate on how to deepen and widen the democratic legitimacy of the EU—debates that are still very much ongoing. The question that the T-Dem is meant to answer is the following: How can we make the eurozone more democratic while sustaining both its effective governance and the integrity of the EU as a whole?

My agreements and disagreements with the T-Dem blueprint stem from my own commitment to what we now refer to as "demoicratic theory" (as opposed to *democratic* theory).[1] The demoicratic constellation of scholars is growing, and it would be impossible to do justice here to the wide range of approaches that it encompasses. Instead I will restate a simple definition and suggest a series of tests for the demoicratization of the eurozone, which I will apply to the proposal at hand.

Democracy, Demoicracy, and Demoicratization

A "demoi-cratic" lens is both a descriptive device to better defend the EU-as-is and a normative device to point to what it ought to aspire to.

For the nature of the beast matters for politics at all times and not least in our era of popular disenchantment with the EU's remoteness and complexity. I believe that citizens cannot perceive the EU as legitimate if they continue to labor under the distortions produced by a kind of mimetic reasoning, assessing it in the same light as a nation-state endowed with a democratically elected government and parliament.

Instead, it makes sense to understand the EU as a *demoicracy*— namely, a "Union of peoples who govern together but not as one" (Nicolaidis 2013). In other words, we should see European democracy as government of peoples exercising self-government in their respective realms, not independently but in an interconnected way. The key to understanding the demoicratic character of the EU is to consider it as a third way, where both of its alternatives—an alliance of sovereigns or a classic federal state—are grounded on the equation between a polity and a single demos. A demoicratic polity, by contrast, primarily values the plurality of interlinked peoples *as interconnected popular sovereigns;* it does not close off or separate each demoi from others or incorporate them into a single demos. As a result, a demoicracy constantly refines ways of sustaining the tension between two concurrent requirements: (i) "autonomy" (referring to the legitimacy of separate, self-determined *demoi;* and (ii) "civicity" (referring to the openness and interconnectedness implied in the notion of liberal democratic *demoi* to whom equal concern is due).

Demoicratic theory is also meant to provide a normative benchmark against which to highlight the EU's pitfalls, thus making clear the vulnerability of its evolving constitutional settlement (Nicolaidis 2018). Crucially, the demoicratic lens reveals the weaknesses of both federal mimetism and sovereignist critiques in its emphasis on the political rather than the ethnic or "essentialist" nature of the demoi in question, and thus on the normative good stemming not only from the autonomy of the demoi but also from their radical openness to each other and mutual accountability. This emphasis on the horizontal or transnational nature of cooperation and delegation over its vertical or supranational dimension is still misunderstood by critics (Wolkenstein 2018). European integration in this sense ought to be understood as an arena for governing together and developing common rules rather than creating a separate and autonomous layer of governance as in classic federations. The point is not that we should restrict the growth of political and social interactions across national borders, but that these should be initiated at the domestic level. Of course, in a stable order of multiple demoi, these demoi cannot exercise popular sovereignty together without accepting certain fundamental, albeit revocable, rules and procedures that must be subject to the familiar democratic tests, such as those of accountability, representation, and institutional checks and balances (Cheneval and Nicolaidis 2016). The normative and political alternatives to a Europe that thrives as a demoicracy are either for it to move backward to become a group of closed demoi or for the demoi to fuse into ever larger sovereign units at ever higher levels of integration.

The concept of *demoicracy* has helped to normatively recast the aspiration for a democratic understanding of Europe's constitutional settlement and has prompted a critical appraisal of paradigms still dominant among European elites (Cheneval and Schimmelfennig 2013; Bellamy 2013; Lindseth 2014; Lacey 2017; Cheneval, Lavenex, and Schimmelfennig 2015). As a theory that seems to correlate transfers of powers with the sustained power of the people, it helps us understand how a union of multiple demoi like the EU ought to handle pressures for deeper integration and further centralization of power as we have witnessed during the eurozone crisis. Demoicratization is the process by which such further integration can be better anchored in the will of the peoples of Europe, as citizens both of particular states and of the EU.

The T-Dem and Demoicracy

In short, the T-Dem proposal stems from a multipronged diagnosis which chimes with that of demoicratic theory.[2]

First, we agree that the crisis of legitimacy induced by the functioning of the EMU—its emergency operation and the ups and down of its reform process—is unprecedented in the EU and needs to be remedied. The EMU touches on areas of policy making that cannot be simply the object of technocratic decision making steered by diplomatic interactions. Indeed, the bulk of EMU reform so far provides the ultimate example of "governance by law," where decisions taken by the EU's executive become entrenched law within the EU without proper legislative scrutiny. Given, in particular, their redistributive impact, these EMU decisions require "authorization" in the fullest sense of the term by popular sovereigns acting through their elected representatives against the backdrop of political debates at all levels. In order to achieve such authorization, Eurocrats—and, more generally, European politicians—will need to overcome their profound suspicion of agonistic (as opposed to antagonistic) politics in the EU, which is grounded in the idea that politics is about open conflicts resolved through democratic competition.

Second, both demoicratic theory and the case for the T-Dem rest on the idea that in the search for democratic anchoring, the constituting polities must take precedence over their supranational expression. The set of substantive social purposes that motivate EU policies come from the bottom up, and it is this *process* of legitimate aggregation of preferences that defines "European peoples," or *demoi,* rather than any ethnic and reified sense of "we." As collectives under a state, the demoi must remain *pouvoir constituant*—whether in their ability to enter, withdraw from, or shape the EU's primary law. When it comes to secondary law, including the management of the EMU, not only do national parliaments need a greater say, but they must be able to express it collectively as well as individually. This would be the case with the Assembly proposed by the T-Dem.

Third, a demoicratic polity is hardly compatible with a policy that allows IMF-type conditionality to become entrenched as something other than an emergency measure (Nicolaidis and Watson 2016). The IMF works (in spite of its own legitimacy deficit) because it is both temporary and external. In contrast, because it has made possible the merger between two hitherto separate logics—namely, the logic of conditionality and that of polity building—the management of the eurozone crisis has allowed the wolf of supranational conditionality to penetrate the EU den. Beyond country programs, witness the European Semester's Macroeconomic Imbalance Procedure (MIP), under which countries can in principle be subject to fines for their failure to take structural measures that, it is assumed, will help reduce their imbalances in the long run. This merger between the conditionality and polity-building logics seeks to make permanent some elements of conditionality that were forged in the heat of the moment as technocratic rather than political solutions to the EMU's woes. Hard cases make bad law, unless great care is taken; and the stress of crisis resolution was not a promising setting in which to shape a new permanent architecture for the EMU (Nicolaidis and Watson 2016). To be sure, the short-run dictates of conditionality are hard to disentangle from enduring requirements in normal times. But conditionality implies an intrusiveness and fosters a divisiveness that do not belong in the operating process of a successful European polity over the long run. Ultimately, the practice of governing at a distance could spell the end of common rules. The T-Dem can contribute to taming the conditionality temptations reigning in Euroland.

Fourth, a demoicratic frame emphasizes the *normative* weight to be given to the quality of horizontal ties, not only between state apparatuses but through transnational networks at all levels (Slaughter 2017). The normative bias of demoicratic scholarship is to shift the spotlight on the imperative of democratic accountability from the vertical focus on internal accountability of liberal theories to horizontal accountability *among* demoi, thus bringing transnationalism all the way down. Demoicratic theory therefore asks how national democratic systems adapt to the imperative of "other-regardingness" or what I call legal empathy, which is at the core of European law (Nicolaidis 2017b). Democratic interdependence—namely, the ways in which democratic processes in different countries affect each other—needs to be managed to ward off an adversarial logic of people versus people. As leaders balance their respective democratic mandates, publics must demand cognitive tools for managing their common demoicratic citizenship (Sternberg, Gartzou-Katsouyanni, and Nicolaidis 2017). The T-Dem proposal can be measured against this requirement to the extent that debates taking place in an interparliamentary Assembly would themselves be embedded in a broader civic pedagogy.

Fifth, when it comes to power, demoicratic theory asks how the *cratos*—the act of "governing together"—avoids the pitfalls of domination, either horizontal domination among between states or vertical domination between EU institutions and the member states. Demoicratic theory focuses its normative gaze on the extent to which power asymmetries are mitigated through (or magnified by) prevailing institutions. The Assembly would potentially contribute to making power visible in the EU, which is a good thing. And to the extent that it would encourage cross-national alliances involving oppositions as well as governments in power, and is linked to potential solidarities across borders, the T-Dem plan would likely help in this regard.

Sixth, demoicratic theory recognizes the crucial importance of commitment strategies in allowing a polity of separate but connected popular sovereignties to be sustainable over time (Moravcsik 1998). But it is also normatively concerned with the foreclosing of options that such commitments create as the product of intergovernmental collusion that might not reflect societal preferences over time and might contribute to the invisibility of power in the EU. Considering the joint decision traps that make it almost impossible to reverse gears in the EU, a demoicratic approach requires much greater use of sunset clauses as well the strengthening of domestic institutions meant to endogenize commitment to outsiders. It would be desirable for the T-Dem to consider the ways in which the Assembly, acting in concert with the rest of eurozone governance, could include sunset clauses in its decision making.

Seventh, and finally, a demoicratic approach takes us beyond interests and into ideas by suggesting that we also need social imaginaries that follow from democratic praxis within and among societies. An incipient demoicratic EU must accommodate a diverse range of imaginings among its citizens of what this polity is, might be, or should be (Lacroix and Nicolaidis 2010; McNamara 2015). Allowing for the coexistence of these diverse perspectives—contrary to the repeated and unimaginative calls for a single European story, including during the 2001–2003 Constitutional Convention—has long enabled a kind of "constructive ambiguity" that has helped avoid entrenched teleological struggles among European political actors. We would need to discuss the ways in which the new T-Dem institutions would allow and even encourage narrative diversity in the EU.

In closing, these considerations imply that the eurozone's democratic credentials are to be judged both by how they affect the qualities and pathologies of national democracies and by how decisions are taken at the center, underscoring the horizontal connection in relations between state and society. The EU must thrive to "do no harm" to its constituent democracies, and its constituent democracies must thrive to continuously improve the rules that allow them to manage both their economic and their political interdependence. Getting national parliaments to work together on EMU management, and to give them the power to do so, is a good start.

But questions remain beyond this basic premise: Why would it be desirable to make representation in the assembly proportional to population at the expense of small countries? What kind of powers ought to be granted to the Assembly that would be compatible with the existing division of labor between (a repatriated) ESM, the ECB, and the Euro-group? Should the appointment of the latter's respective presidents not be the object of systematic consensus building with the Council? Are the provisions envisaged sufficiently clear on the division of labor between the Assembly and the European Parliament? How to deal with the inevitable conflicts that may arise? Would these proposals allow for replacing the conditionality drift within EMU with more sustainable and long-term political bargains? How would externalities between this Assembly and the rest of the EU be managed? The T-Dem proposal does not pretend to offer answers to all questions, but it has the great merit of encouraging us to raise them under a new light.

Notes

1. The term "demoicracy" is derived from demoi (δῆμοι in original ancient Greek is the plural form of δῆμος), meaning "peoples," and kratos (κράτος), meaning "power"—or "to govern oneself with strength." Peoples here are understood both individually, as citizens who happen to be born or reside in the territory of the Union, and collectively as states—the separate political units under popular sovereignty that constitute the Union.
2. Some of what follows is drawn from Nicolaidis 2018.

References

Begg, Iain, Annette Bongardt, Kalypso Nicolaidis, and Francisco Torres. 2015. "EMU and Sustainable Integration," *Journal of European Integration* 37 (7) (November).

Bellamy, Richard. "'An Ever Closer Union Aaong the Peoples of Europe': Republican Intergovernmentalism and Demoicratic Representation within the EU," *Journal of European Integration* 35, no. 5 (2013): 499–516.

Chalmers, D., M. Jachtenfuchs, and C. Joerges, eds. 2016. *The End of the Eurocrats' Dream.* Cambridge: Cambridge University Press.

Cheneval, Francis. 2011. *The Government of the Peoples: On the Idea and Principles of Multilateral Democracy.* New York: Palgrave MacMillan.

Cheneval, Francis, Sandra Lavenex, and Frank Schimmelfennig. 2015. "Demoi-cracy in the European Union: Principles, Institutions, Policies," *Journal of European Public Policy* 22 (1).

Cheneval, Francis, and Kalypso Nicolaidis. 2016. "The Social Construction of Demoicracy in the EU," *European Journal of Political Theory* (Spring).

Cheneval, Francis, and Frank Schimmelfennig. "The Case forDemoicracy in the European Union," *JCMS: Journal of Common Market Studies* 51, no. 2 (2013): 334–350.

Lacey, Joseph. *Centripetal Democracy: Democratic Legitimacy and Political Identity in Belgium, Switzerland, and the European Union.* Oxford: Oxford University Press, 2017.

Lacroix, Justine, and Kalypso Nicolaïdis, eds. *European Stories: Intellectual Debates on Europe in National Contexts.* Oxford: Oxford University Press, 2010.

Lindseth, Peter L. *Power and Legitimacy: Reconciling Europe and the Nation-State.* Oxford: Oxford University Press, 2010.

McNamara, K. R. 2015. *The Politics of Everyday Europe: Constructing Authority in the European Union.* New York: Oxford University Press.

Moravcsik, A. 1998. *The Choice for Europe: Social Purpose and State Power from Messina to Maastricht.* Ithaca, NY: Cornell University Press, 1998.

Nicolaidis, Kalypso. 2004. "We the Peoples of Europe," *Foreign Affairs* 83 (6): 97–110.

———. 2012. "The Idea of European Demoicracy." In *Philosophical Foundations of European Union Law,* edited by Julie Dickson and Pavlos Eleftheriadis. Oxford: Oxford University Press.

———. 2013. "European Demoicracy and Its Crisis," *Journal of Common Market Studies* 51 (2) (March): 351–369.

———. 2017a. "Mutual Recognition: Promise and Denial, from Sapiens to Brexit," *Current Legal Problems* (December).

———. 2017b. "Sustainable Integration in a Demoicratic Polity: A New (or Not So New) Ambition for the European Union after Brexit." In *Brexit and Beyond,* edited by Uta Staiger. Cambridge: Cambridge University Press.

———. 2018. "Braving the Waves? Europe's Constitutional Settlement at 20," *Journal of Common Market Studies* (December).

Nicolaidis, Kalypso, and Max Watson. 2016. "Sharing the Eurocrats' Dream: A Demoi-cratic Approach to EMU Governance in the Post-Crisis Era." In *The End of the Eurocrat's Dream,* edited by Damian Chalmers, Markus Jachtenfuchs, and Christian Joerges. Cambridge: Cambridge University Press.

Slaughter, A. M. (2017). *The Chessboard and the Web: Strategies of Connection in a Networked World.* New Haven, CT: Yale University Press.

Sternberg, C., Kira Gartzou-Katsouyanni, and Kalypso Nicolaidis. 2017. *Mutual Recognition Lost: The Greco-German Affair in the Euro-Crisis.* Oxford: Palgrave-Macmillan.

Van Middelaar, Luuk. 2013. *The Passage to Europe: How a Continent Became a Union.* New Haven, CT: Yale University Press.

Wolkenstein, Fabio. "Demoicracy, Transnational Partisanship and the EU," *JCMS: Journal of Common Market Studies* 56, no. 2 (2018): 284–299.

10

The European Parliament Is the Parliament of the Euro Area

PIERRE MOSCOVICI

D ebate is what invigorates the European project. I have traveled the length and the breadth of Europe, in both a personal and a professional capacity, and it seems that everyone has an opinion on what needs to be done to revitalize the EU. Perhaps the most important element of this debate involves the euro area. Here, the elephant has been in the room for some time and it can no longer be ignored. The decision-making process in the euro area is plagued by a glaring deficit of democratic legitimacy. I have observed this firsthand in the Eurogroup over many years, first as France's minister of finance and then as European Commissioner for Economic and Financial Affairs.

In its most extreme manifestation, this democratic deficit has had the result of depriving countries under financial assistance of an essential part of their economic sovereignty. Of course, the case of Greece is the most egregious, with severe social consequences. Furthermore, the current structure ensures that competing national interests within the Eurogroup will always take precedence over European interests. This is compounded by the European Commission's weak institutional position within the (informal) Eurogroup, with the result that European interests have no representation.

It has become increasingly clear that the current system allows some national parliaments a much greater say in the decision-making process than others. National chambers such as the Bundestag that give a precise mandate to their finance minister have a decisive sway on the decisions of the Eurogroup. In practice, today there are first- and second-class national parliaments in the euro area, and the combination of red lines drawn by the former drastically reduces the scope of possibilities in the Eurogroup.

Central to the issue is the question of accountability. Although finance ministers may be accountable to their national parliaments, they are not accountable to the European Parliament for the decisions made collectively in the Eurogroup. Furthermore, there is very little transparency throughout the decision-making process.

Finally, the significant powers of oversight afforded to the EU level as regards national economic policy making, and in particular national budgets, are not matched with a proportionate degree of democratic control at the same level. My assessment last year, that there is a "democratic scandal" in our institutional setup, remains the same. However, while I agree entirely with Thomas Piketty's diagnosis, I differ on the remedy.

My American friends understand better than most the complexities involved with bringing together states, and therefore competing interests, to form a federal structure. The European project has always been, and will always be, based on the consent of the various peoples that make up our Union, as expressed through their national parliaments. No matter how perfect a democracy we can build at the supranational level, it will never trump the legitimacy of national parliaments. Brexit, of course, was a most regrettable reminder of this. Democracy, however, is desirable in itself, as a matter of principle: that is a strong enough rationale to pursue more democracy at the European level.

I have followed Thomas Piketty's proposal for a euro-area Assembly with interest. Naturally, I can see the appeal of a dramatic overhaul of our economic governance. Yet I can also see how unrealistic it is to hope for such an overhaul in the immediate future. In the short term, our priority needs to be to build on what exists and improve it. If a European *demos* has to emerge and supersede the national *demos* as a prerequisite to improve democratic control and accountability in the EU, then we may as well give up: populists will take over.

We need to be pragmatic. To return to the American example, the pragmatism that has characterized American federalism can offer us some inspiration as we reflect on possible short- to medium-term solutions. It is always possible to draw from other institutional models without mimicking them. The EU is, and will remain, a *sui generis* construct for the decades to come.

Needless to say, the cacophony of competing national interests that often characterizes Eurogroup meetings results in suboptimal policy making. The objective of any reform must therefore be to ensure greater harmony between competing national interests. Only then will the whole be greater than the sum of its parts.

In order to achieve this goal, we must have real, meaningful democratic reform of the Eurogroup. We must then look at developing new tools at the EU level to defuse confrontations between diverging national interests.

Any reform must take into account the current economic architecture of the euro area. We have a monetary policy that is independent today, and must remain so. Furthermore, reform must operate within the bounds of the current mechanisms for preventive economic and fiscal coordination between members of the euro area (which combine complex rules and discretionary powers exercised by the European Commission). The limited EU competence over taxation, and the unanimous voting rules in this area, mean that there is currently little coordination on tax and social policies. Finally, the current framework provides for financial assistance for member states only in very serious situations, accompanied by a confiscation of some level of national sovereignty from the member state receiving it.

These are the rules of the game, and will remain so for the immediate future. Any action to enhance the democratic dimension of the euro area must respect this framework.

Injecting More Democracy into the Eurogroup

The argument that national parliaments must be more involved in the euro area's decision-making process (given that real democratic legitimacy will remain at the national level for the foreseeable future) is at first sight compelling. A euro-area Assembly, a sort of "chamber of national chambers," would certainly provide national parliaments with greater oversight than they currently have. Yet such a proposal has clear limitations; specifically, it is difficult to see how it would help define and promote the European interest. Furthermore, it is likely that such an approach would result in a "self-locking democracy" where conflicts between diverging national interests within the Eurogroup are merely mirrored in, and amplified by, similar conflicts emanating from national parliaments.

Besides, agreeing on the makeup of a new parliamentary chamber composed of representatives of national parliaments would not be an easy task. Additionally, decision making would be unlikely to be any simpler or more transparent than it currently is in the European Parliament. For example, how would German socialists participating in a grand coalition at the federal level vote on an initiative inspired by conservative parties? Would they betray their political family or their coalition partners?

This vision also overlooks the unique role of the European Commission. It is the Commission's responsibility to ensure that each member of the euro area fulfills its commitments. This is a crucial role in a system that relies on mutual trust between member states as a prerequisite for solidarity. The Commission is the only body in a position to promote the general European interest.

Some will agree that a stronger role is needed for the central level, but that the legitimacy of the central power will stem from the "predictability" of its decisions. They will typically argue for more technocratic automaticity as a guarantee for rules to be unwaveringly implemented.

It is not the exercise of discretionary powers that undermines the legitimacy of the Eurogroup. Rather, it is the absence of democratic control over these powers. In my view the Commission should maintain and possibly even expand its discretionary powers on matters of economic and fiscal coordination. This should be accompanied by stronger democratic accountability and control. In other words, the Commission's role must be improved and subject to appropriate oversight, not replaced.

Bearing this in mind, how can we inject more democracy into the Eurogroup?

We need to shed light on the inner workings of the Eurogroup. This is required not only for the sake of transparency but because scrutiny will influence the outcome of crucial decisions. Hence the need for a "euro-area finance minister" who would have a "double-hat" (chairing both the Eurogroup as well as being a member of the European Commission). Decisions made in the Eurogroup should be subject to proper oversight by Europe's elected representatives. As things stand, only European Commissioners are accountable to the European Parliament. Finance ministers, including the president of the Eurogroup, are not.

The euro-area finance minister should be *individually* accountable to the European Parliament. For instance, the president of the European Commission could politically commit to allocate another portfolio to the euro-area finance minister within the College of Commissioners, should the European Parliament hold a vote of no-confidence (with a qualified majority—such as three-fifths of MEPs) on the minister. The European Parliament could also decide to meet in a "euro-area format" for matters pertaining to the Economic and Monetary Union—at least for as long as the euro is the currency of a subset of member states.

Double-hatting, individual accountability of the euro-area finance minister, and a euro-area format within the European Parliament are all institutional innovations that can be implemented in the short term and do not require treaty change. These reforms would go a long way to enhance democratic control and accountability in the EMU. Furthermore, all they require is political will.

Developing New Tools at the Central Level to Defuse Confrontations between Diverging National Interests

In addition to enhancing democratic control and accountability, it is also necessary to develop new tools at the central level to defuse confrontations between diverging national interests. Such tools are vital in order to stabilize the economic cycle in the euro area and finance policies that enhance cohesion, convergence and the reduction of inequalities within and between member states, *without further encroaching on the prerogatives of national parliaments.*

In a sense, the current mechanisms of economic and fiscal coordination in the euro area represent the worst of both worlds. National sovereignty is undermined, yet the system remains ineffective. In other words, national parliaments do not maintain full control over their budgets, nor is there a European veto over national budgets (and nor should there be!) if they run against the interests of the euro area. No one can compel the Dutch or German Parliaments to vote for a budget that would reduce their current account surpluses. Nor can anyone prevent the Italian or French Parliaments from adopting a budget deficit.

New instruments can safeguard the European interest without further eroding national sovereignty.

Remaining concerns about the viability of the common currency will not be assuaged by further centralizing powers to scrutinize national fiscal policies. Only a euro-area budget (sufficiently large and independently managed) will support less pro-cyclical fiscal policies. We cannot (and should not) compel national parliaments to run less pro-cyclical fiscal policies; but we can develop tools at the European level that would serve this purpose.

The 2019 European elections will offer a unique opportunity to discuss these questions publically. If properly organized, they will also provide the chance to deepen the democratic dimension of the European Union. The appointment of *Spitzenkandidaten* by European parties (a recent and still fragile innovation) and a first transnational list to fill the seats left vacant by (a still to be finalized) Brexit are all steps toward a more democratic Europe. 2019 can be a turning point for European democracy.

11

A Eurozone Congress

LUUK VAN MIDDELAAR AND VESTERT BORGER

B etween spring 2010 and summer 2012, the euro was at least three times close to collapsing, but in a sustained effort of firefighting and improvisation, European Union leaders and institutions managed to save it. Five years after the emergency, public support for the currency zone is again solid. Especially Emmanuel Macron's victory in the 2017 French election has reenergized ideas for reforming the monetary union, even if operational follow-up has to wait for German coalition building. This lull is a good moment for reflection on the euro's democratic future.

The European Commission, stepping into the debate in December 2017 with a series of proposals, wishes to prune the eurozone of its messy branches and strange crisis outgrowths. It aims to bring the rescue funds of the European Stability Mechanism (ESM) within the Treaty remit as a European IMF, to "repatriate" the Fiscal Compact, and to give the Eurogroup of Finance Ministers a permanent chair who also is a Commission vice president and hence accountable to the Parliament— all in the name of efficiency and democracy.[1] Unsurprisingly, the Juncker Commission rejects ideas of a separate eurozone parliament.[2] Such a body upsets the Brussels doctrine; this is true for both the "Macron" MEPs-only variant and perhaps even more for the T-Dem composite version.

Whereas the Commission prefers to treat currency politics as just any other Union policy, the authors of T-Dem rightly contend in the Intro- duction to the present volume: "Governing the euro area is not like governing Europe in the past: it is no longer about organizing a common market, it is now about coordinating economic policies, harmonizing tax systems, and fostering convergence among national budgetary policies, thereby entering the very heart of member states' social contracts."

Most of the economic and budgetary policy competences have until now remained in the hands of the member states, and for good reason. At the same time, the crisis made clear to the public at large that the euro is also a common good. The eurozone becomes stronger if this specific nature of its politics is acknowledged.

We therefore warmly welcome the T-Dem proposal for a eurozone assembly composed of national and European parliamentarians. We also agree with the authors that such a body should have substantial powers in order not to become a "talking shop." We argue below that it should concentrate on the newly emerged highest political authority in the currency union, serving in fact more as a "Eurozone Congress"; for both political and constitutional reasons, its powers should not interfere in the already crowded field of European and national lawmaking, by setting the corporate tax rate and pool public debt; and its purpose might be better served with a legal basis in the Union Treaties, instead of a new treaty.

Summit and Congress

Since the negotiations on the Treaty of Maastricht, some member states, in particular France, have stressed the need for a *gouvernement économique*, a highest political authority for the currency union, embodied by the heads of state or government. Due to resistance of other member states, in particular Germany, these efforts have not found their way into the Union Treaties. Hence, the finance ministers, halfway between the technical and political levels, were attributed most powers in coordinating economic and budgetary policies (arts. 121, 126 TFEU).

The financial and sovereign debt crises have exposed the shortcomings of this arrangement. As of 2008, at the initiative of French president Sarkozy, the political vacuum has been "filled" by the Euro Summit. From an *ad hoc* meeting at the height of the banking crisis to a series of "summits of the truth" in 2010 and 2011, it was accorded legal recognition in the 2012 Fiscal Compact.[3] In the line of authority, the Euro

Summit takes precedence over the Eurogroup, as became very visible for the public at large during the more recent Greek debt saga in the summer of 2015. But it was no different during earlier key episodes in the crisis.[4] In emergencies and for strategic decisions, the "chiefs" are in charge, either in full European Council format or in euro-area composition. Contrary to what the author of the T-Dem argue, it is therefore the joint presidents and prime ministers in their various constellations who bear primary responsibility for eurozone politics vis-à-vis their electorates.

The creation of the Summit forms an expression of the political nature of the currency union, where national economic policies and central steering go hand in hand. Some observers conclude that the currency union, in its present form, cannot survive: that it should develop into a federal entity or it will collapse. We don't share this view. The blend of national and central features corresponds to the European Union's constitutional nature, in which constituent power lies with the member states whose governments also play a central role at the level of constituted power. This is a historical and political reality that governments are aware of, but that is often missed, or dismissed, by economic commentators and legal scholars. And yet political leaders in this setup not only act on their own national interests, but also in concert, in support of the common good, as representatives of *member* states.[5]

This political awareness at the executive level of a common bond is difficult to create or reproduce at the level of democratic representation and control. National leaders sit around the same table; national parliamentarians do not. Hence the present conundrum, in which neither the European Parliament nor the national parliaments are capable of adequately acting in this "intermediate sphere," where national and common interests meet.[6] This is the source of the "blind spot" the authors identify in the Introduction to this volume, and this is where their case for a eurozone parliament, with its composite membership, is strongest. The body would control the political decisions that the Euro Summit takes, such as the green-lighting of financial assistance, the initiation of new constructs like the Banking Union, the setting of economic priorities, and personnel issues such as the nomination of the Eurogroup president, who should become a full-time chair.

In light of its major interlocutor and its dual composition, this Parliamentary Assembly should perhaps not be called the "Eurozone

Parliament" but instead the "Eurozone Congress." Already in 2003 then European Convention president Valéry Giscard d'Estaing coined the term "European Congress" for an assembly consisting of national and European parliamentarians that would gather for important occasions.[7] But whereas the body envisaged by Giscard would be little more than an applauding machine, legitimizing the authority of the European Council and its president, the Eurozone Congress would have teeth.

In sum, the Eurozone Congress should operate as the parliamentary interlocutor of the "chiefs." Their political decisions or strategic orientations would require its consent.

Ministers and Congress

The Eurogroup stands below the Summit in the line of authority. Under the radar, it has witnessed a major increase in its powers. It no longer operates only as an informal body;[8] it also takes legally binding decisions when its members meet in their capacity as governors of the permanent rescue fund, the ESM.[9] The governors approve of assistance and its payment in tranches, control the drafting of memorandums of understanding, and decide on increases in the capital of the fund.[10] Here too, there is no adequate joint parliamentary control and there is a role to play for the Eurozone Congress. In our view this role would still exist if and when the ESM would be "repatriated" in the Union Treaties. The politics of the currency union, after all, would continue to demand dual legitimacy.

However, we do not agree that the eurozone assembly, acting as "legislator" together with the Eurogroup, should acquire competences allowing it to set the corporate tax rate or to pool public debt (arts. 12(2)–(4) T-Dem). That would go way beyond addressing the democratic "blind spot." It would amount to a fundamental change in the division of responsibilities between the national level and the central level. In this regard the authors make no secret of their wish to break Germany's hold on the direction of economic policy, spelling out the Assembly's capacity to outvote a recalcitrant bloc of German deputies. This is surprising, because they themselves assert in the Introduction to this volume that they wish to avoid a situation in which "the institutions of a national democracy operate in a vacuous space." This move cannot be compensated by "associating" national parliamentarians, in their capacity as members of the Congress, with such decisions. It would bereave national parliaments of a vital power, and thus meet with political as well as constitutional obstacles and concerns.

In sum, the Eurozone Congress could also act as the parliamentary interlocutor of euro-area finance ministers, be it in the forum of the Eurogroup or in the ESM Board of Governors, and in particular of their full-time president (who, in our view, should not also be a Commission vice president). This in itself warrants its existence, but it requires no major transfer of budgetary competences—which in practice would be a major hurdle to its coming about.

Treaties and Congress

How to establish the eurozone assembly? The authors of T-Dem opt for a new treaty. And they have the law on their side. Member states can exercise their economic policy competences individually but also jointly, through the conclusion of an international treaty, as was (re)confirmed by the European Court in *Pringle* when it approved of the ESM.[11] But what are the benefits of this approach over amendment of the Union Treaties? The authors argue that the latter is an arduous process as it requires the consent of all member states, yet the conclusion of a new treaty is not without obstacles either. Such a treaty also needs to be approved and ratified by the eurozone states in line with their constitutional requirements, which means that it may become the subject of a referendum, as happened with the Fiscal Compact in Ireland, or a constitutional challenge, notably in Germany. Because the hurdles to the establishment of a eurozone assembly will consequently be significant anyhow, it is best to take the royal road: amendment of the Union Treaties.

This is not to say that we reject the use of international treaties altogether. During the crisis it proved a valuable tool when the situation called for *instant action*. The argument that there is some democratic urgency has its appeal but cannot be equated with moments of sheer survival.

To Conclude

Establishing a Eurozone Congress will not be easy. Neither proud national parliaments nor the prickly European Parliament like to see new
rivals on their turf. The authors seem to underestimate this potential
for on-the-ground resistance (which has effectively killed the interparliamentary forum foreseen by Article 13 of the Fiscal Compact). The best
way to overcome this resistance to its creation is to stress the complementary nature of the Congress.

In many cases existing institutions can adapt to the demands of a
new situation. In general, prudence is therefore in order before engaging
in institutional engineering. But the authors are fully right that the existing parliaments have not been able to fill the void of democratic control, and—we would add—are unlikely to do so in the near future. Their
case for a eurozone assembly is therefore strong.

The Eurozone Congress would be a forum bringing together the
various debates *in* and *on* the currency union, which now often take
place within the confines of national boundaries. But the objective of
energizing the political debate should not be confounded with achieving
certain policy outcomes. At some points the T-Dem authors seem to favor
the latter over the former, emphasizing the chance for the Left to depart from the "politics of austerity" of the crisis years. The beauty of the
Congress, however, lies in its representative function, as both echo
chamber and a place forging a stronger common bond. It would be a pity
to preempt and close these functions of openness by ascribing it an *a
priori* economic destination.

Notes

1. European Commission, "Further Steps towards Completing Europe's Economic and Monetary Union: A Roadmap," Brussels, December 6, 2017, COM
   (2017)821.
2. In his September 2017 State of the Union speech, Juncker said: "The parliament for the eurozone is the European Parliament." (His Strasbourg
   audience applauded.)
3. Art. 12, Fiscal Compact.

4. See, in this regard, Luuk van Middelaar, *De nieuwe politiek van Europa* (Historische Uitgeverij, 2017), pp. 256–259 (discussing the involvement of political leaders in the Cypriot assistance operation of 2013); and Vestert Borger, *The Transformation of the Euro: Law, Contract, Solidarity* (diss., Leiden University,2018), §5.3 (discussing the steering role of the leaders in relation to the establishment of the temporary rescue facilities EFSF and EFSM in the weekend of May 7–9, 2010).

5. Either through institutions like the European Council or through international agreements like the Fiscal Compact or the ESM Treaty.

6. This is a key argument in Luuk van Middelaar, *The Passage to Europe: How a Continent Became a Union* (Yale University Press, 2013).

7. Note that one could argue that the Union's constitutional setup already contains a (legislative) "Congress," consisting of the Council and the European Parliament.

8. Strictly speaking, the Eurogroup *de facto* also has the capacity to adopt legally binding decisions under the Union Treaties, because states outside the currency union are excluded from voting in the Council on certain economic policy decisions (see arts. 139(2) and 139(4), TFEU).

9. Art. 5, ESM Treaty.

10. Since the entry into force of the "Two-Pack," the main elements of economic policy conditionality linked to ESM assistance also have to be approved by the Council (see art. 7, reg. 472 / 2013).

11. Case C-370 / 12 *Pringle* [2012]ECLI:EU:C:2012:756.

12

The Economy Is a Polity

Implications for the New Modes of Economic Governance in the EU

CHRISTIAN JOERGES

The Main Concerns of the T-Dem Initiative

The explanatory statement to the Draft Treaty on the Democratization of the Governance of the Euro Area summarizes in less than 1,000 words the uneasiness with the *praxis* of European crisis politics.[1] The outrageousness that Böckenförde observed back in 2010 has become a trademark of a plethora of measures taken since then.[2] Suffice it here to emphasize three points:

(1) The first concerns the equality and political dignity of the member states of the EU. This is a principle that defines the Union as Union. Sadly and tellingly, not only has it been disregarded by European politics, but it has also—in particular—been neglected by the German Constitutional Court in its judgment on the rescue package for Greece of September 11, 2011,[3] where the Court defended the budgetary power of the German Bundestag while, by the same token, not caring at all for the rights of the Greek Parliament.[4] More widely noticed are the measures—all too euphemistically called memorandums of understanding. To be sure, they were legalized by the amendment of Art. 136 TFEU in 2011.[5] My point here is that the *praxis* of conditionality is irreconcilable with the

foundational values of the European project. Europe is not to transform the principles of equality, mutual respect, and cooperation into command-and-control relationships. This constitutes an unacceptable intrusion into the practice of democratic political will-formation.[6]

(2) Democracy was not, and could not be, in the DNA of the Treaty of Rome and the EEC. However, it has been a shared understanding throughout both the affirmative and the critical assessment of the technocratic legacy of the integration project that Europe must not pervert democratic constitutionalism into technocratic rule. It has to justify, and, by the same token, delimit the resort to nonmajoritarian institutions. The executive summary highlights a significant strengthening of the executive capacity of European institutions in the field of economic policy. The upshot here is the strengthening of the power of the European Central Bank. The assumption that the Bank or the European System of Central Banks—which is not legitimated by a democratic vote and cannot be held accountable by Europe's citizens—can be empowered to take far-reaching distributional decisions and intervene, even if only indirectly or behind a veil of public inattention, in policy fields in which the Union lacks powers, is simply indefensible.[7]

(3) A comprehensive list of queries would be much longer.[8] The *de facto* by far most important means by which the constitutional transformation was accomplished was the replacement of the Community method by what the German chancellor has characterized as the Union method. To be sure, resort to international law has occurred throughout the history of the integration project. However, it has never been so spectacular and so obviously beyond the Union's commitments to the rule of law and democracy.

The Union method is for very good reasons the focus of the explanatory memorandum. The response to it is a U-turn: "the 'T-Dem' replicates the *modus operandi* of both the TSCG and the ESM Treaty (as validated by the Court of Justice of the European Union in its *Pringle* ruling from November 2012) to address the financial crisis, but does so in order to engage in a democratizing effort."[9] Alternative conditionality is the submitted alternative to the TINA (There Is No Alternative) message repeated *ad nauseam* by Chancellor Merkel throughout the long years of crisis politics. It is a response with analytical and normative strength. This strength stems from the implicit acknowledgment that the financial crisis has generated an emergency.[10] Quite obviously, a "return to the rules" as they had been established prior to the crisis is, in view of the design defects of the Maastricht Treaty and its Economic and Monetary Union, undesirable and, after nearly a decade of hectic activities and the production of hundreds of pages of legal texts, inconceivable.[11] The EMU cannot be made undone—but it can be changed! It cannot be made undone, but it can be changed. This message is encouraging. But how about its normative credentials and its political realism?

Europe in Troubled Waters—Is More Europe the Solution?

The life of the integration project has been a life with crises that at the end have always strengthened the Union. We know this mantra. Whenever Europe is in difficulties, the proper reaction has always been and should be: more Europe. What sounds so familiar has become essentially unbelievable. The cascade of crises to which we are exposed is of such magnitude and depth that we cannot count on some miraculous constitutional moment but should first expose ourselves to a theoretical moment, long enough to discuss intensively the conditions and prospects of a reinvention of our project. Pertinent efforts are under way. The one on which I focus in the following remarks is Daniel Innerarity's *Philosophy of the European Union,* because of both the inherent qualities of this study and also because of its theoretical orientation.[12] Innerarity's ambition resonates perfectly well with the intentions of the T-Dem initiative. He provides us with a new vision of the future of democracy in the Union. However, this is by no means a one-sided relationship. The T-Dem may open avenues for a realization of this Philosophy of the European Union.

The indicators of such complementarity are manifold. Among the countless proposals for the future of Europe, the T-Dem is the one most credibly pursuing a commitment to democracy. This credibility stems from the exposure of all the involved disciplines—law, political science, sociology, even economics—to democratic values and claims. In its institutional suggestions, the T-Dem proposal takes up the main concerns of the critics—namely, the critique of technocratic rule with its pretense to infallible or incontestable, sacrosanct expert knowledge; the insolation of this type of rule against democratic objections and accountability claims by the establishment of a cooperative parliamentary body (the "Parliamentary Assembly of the Euro Area" entrusted with "the final say on the vote of the euro-area budget, the base and rate of corporate tax, and any other legislative act foreseen by the T-Dem").[13] As already underlined, the idea of an alternative conditionality does not seek to do away with the coordination within European economic governance, but exposes its exercise to political contestation and requirements of democratic accountability.

Daniel Innerarity's *Philosophy of the European Union* operates on more abstract theoretical levels and over much longer time horizons. His analysis is not restricted to the last decade but identifies a series of deficiencies of the integration project, which were partly dormant for a long time and partly triggered by the conflict constellations of the recent crises. Innerarity is, of course, not the first philosopher to build bridges between the debates on Europe as they unfold in the various disciplines—law, political science, sociology, political economy—and philosophical enquiries into the legitimacy of a transnational polity. His philosophical agenda is, in significant aspects, indebted to the Habermasian theory of deliberative democracy and Habermas's anti-technocratic normativism. However, he is much more specific and realistic in his democratic visions than Habermas, given the latter's ideas about dual national and European citizenship as the basis and source of a transnational European democracy.[14] Throughout his discussion of the various dimensions of the *problématique* of a democratization of Europe, Innerarity underlines that this project must do justice to both the complexity of the European system and the interdependencies the integration process has generated. The message of the book throughout the whole range of issues that it addresses is inspired by the analytical and normative implications of these insights: the complexity of Europeanization has a democratic potential, which needs to be spelled out analytically and used politically. Implicit in this message is a critical stance. The lack of such perspectives in so many domains of European studies contributes to their fallacies and impasses in their responses to the critical state of the EU and of transnational governance in general.

In these perceptions, Innerarity's arguments display significant affinities with the T-Dem. What we are witnessing today is a regressive reestablishment of strict disciplinary boundaries. Economists have become the principal advisors of political leaders, and they tend to restrict themselves to functionalist arguments; political scientists try to polish up their outlived integration theories; lawyers forget about the normative *proprium* of their medium and content themselves with meticulous descriptive accounts of ongoing transformations. Under such conditions, a philosophical voice that insists on the need for renewed analytics and concepts is a valuable interlocutor for the protagonists of a democratic conditionality—who will appreciate Innerarity's normative concerns and can draw upon their institutional suggestions in the further elaboration of his visions.

No Alternative?

Should all of these affinities imply a common deficiency when reminded of Hegel's *Ohnmacht des Sollens* (The powerlessness of the ought)? Such concerns must indeed be taken seriously. They can be specified with the help of a passage from Karl Polanyi's *Grand Transformation*. What Polanyi tried to explain was the destruction of liberal economic ordering by Fascism and Nazism. However, the end of the Second World War nurtured hopes for a better national and international future:

> With the disappearance of the automatic mechanism of the gold standard, governments will find it possible to . . . tolerate willingly that other nations shape their domestic institutions according to their inclinations, thus transcending the pernicious nineteenth century dogma of the necessary uniformity of domestic regimes within the orbit of world economy. Out of the ruins of the Old World, cornerstones of the New can be seen to emerge: economic collaboration of governments *and* the liberty to organize national life at will.[15]

The passage is extraordinary for three reasons. For one, it replicates the Polanyian argument that the capitalist market economy is not an evolutionary accomplishment, let alone an autonomously functioning machine, but a political product—"*laissez-faire* was planned"[16]—which requires institutional backing and continuous political management. "The political" is inherent in "the economic"—markets are "polities."[17] A second insight follows from this: There will be a variety of capitalist market economies, which mirror a variety of political preferences and socioeconomic conditions. This is what Polanyi means when he says that our societies enjoy the "liberty to organize national life at will. The third is only alluded to in half a sentence: Polanyi advocates a "collaboration of governments." This is a political vision below or beyond the elimination of divergences. Let us first glance briefly at the second insight.

Since Peter A. Hall and David Soskice initiated the "varieties of capitalism" studies in 2011, Polanyi's second point has become common knowledge. These studies both confirm and underline that market economies do not operate uniformly because their institutional configurations vary significantly. What the studies neglect are ideational commitments—the cultural traditions and normative aspects that accompany and orient the ordering of the economy.[18] Both the authors of the Draft Treaty on the Democratization of the Governance of the Euro Area and Daniel Innerarity in his *Political Theory of the EU* seem in this respect to be more sensitive. Be that as it may, I do believe that these aspects have to be taken into account. They are, in my view, indispensable elements of an adequate understanding of the economic, particularly in view of the diversities within the European space. The work of economic historians such as Werner Abelshauser and the pathbreaking comparative law studies of Gunther Teubner emphasize that culture tends to be remarkably resistant to imposed change.[19] Both underline that interventions into the respective social and institutional fabric of European economies can hardly be subtle and fine-tuned enough to accomplish the desired reorientation.[20]

Against this background, the difficulties of European crisis politics—with its imposition of structural convergence of the southern with the northern economies of the eurozone—is anything but surprising. There is a normative side to these historical, sociological, and legal findings: command-and-control interventions, which are guided by the presumption that one size will fit all, are accompanied by the risk of destructive effects. The imposition of changes with disintegrative impact is not only unwise but also illegitimate. I submit that the normative fabric of the economic orders within member states on which the proper functioning of their economies rests deserves to be recognized as a "*social acquis.*"[21] The *social acquis* is a moving target. To respect it would mean, not to petrify national constellation, but to strengthen the political autonomy of the political preferences and social orientations that are generated and formed by specific historical experiences, political contestation, and societal learning and continuous political decision making. It has to be added that the *social acquis* has been threatened not only by the European crisis politics of 2007–2008 but also by the jurisprudence of the CJEU, which shortly before the beginning of the financial crisis subjected the labor law and related welfare of the member states to the economic freedoms.[22] A protection of the *social acquis* would require European judicial restraint in labor-law issues, which, according to the Treaty, remain a prerogative of the member states.[23]

Further queries follow from this. One concerns the effect of democratization. The opening up of by-now authoritatively ordered vertical and horizontal conflict constellations in the realms of economic and financial policies would lay bare conflicts of interests and of policy preferences among the affected national and European actors and institutions. It is the specific characteristic of democratic processes and political contestation that their outcomes are unpredictable. It seems also quite likely that such openness would require a loosening of the disciplining powers of the common currency.[24] The unwillingness to embark on such an uncharted sea, however, is by no means a guarantee for political and social peace, not even for economic stability.[25]

Notes

1. Explanatory statement to the Draft Treaty on the Democratization of the Governance of the Euro Area, available at piketty.pse.ens.fr.
2. E.-W. Böckenförde, "Kennt die europäische Not kein Gebot? Die Webfehler der EU und die Notwendigkeit einer neuen politischen Entscheidung," *Neue Züricher Zeitung*, June 21, 2010, p. 305 *et seq.*
3. German Federal Constitutional Court, judgment of November 7, 2011, 2 BvR 987 / 10.
4. C. Joerges, "Der Berg kreißte—gebar er eine Maus? Europa vor dem Bundesverfassungsgericht," *WSI-Mitteilungen* 65, no. 8 (2012): 560; M. Everson, "An Exercise in Legal Honesty: Rewriting the Court of Justice and the Bundesverfassungsgericht," *European Law Journal* 21, no. 4 (2015): 474 *et seq.*
5. European Council Decision of March 25, 2011, amending art. 136 of the Treaty on the Functioning of the European Union with regard to a stability mechanism for member states whose currency is the euro. Art. 1, para. 3: "The member states whose currency is the euro may establish a stability mechanism to be activated if indispensable to safeguard the stability of the euro area as a whole. The granting of any required financial assistance under the mechanism will be made subject to strict conditionality."

6. A. Albi, "Erosion of Constitutional Rights in EU Law: A Call for 'Substantive Co-Operative Constitutionalism,'" *Vienna Journal of International Constitutional Law* 9, no. 2 (2015): 151 *et seq.*

7. J. White, *Authority after Emergency Rule,* in *Modern Law Review,* 2015, p. 589.

8. C. Joerges, "Pereat iustitia, fiat mundus: What Is Left of the European Economic Constitution after the OMT-Litigation," *Maastricht Journal of European and Comparative Law* 23, no. 1 (2016: 112–116.

9. Explanatory statement, 2.

10. Böckenförde's (see *supra,* note 2) reference to this category is by now no longer exceptional; cf. K. Dyson, "Sworn to Grim Necessity? Imperfections of European Economic Governance, Normative Political Theory, and Supreme Emergency," *Journal of European Integration* 35, no. 3 (2013): 207 *et seq.*; J. White, "Emergency Europe," in *Political Studies* 63, no. 2 (2015): 659 *et seq.*; C. Kilpatrick, "On the Rule of Law and Economic Emergency: The Degradation of Basic Legal Values in Europe's Bailouts," *Oxford Journal of Legal Studies* 35, no. 2 (2015): 325 *et seq.*; C. Kreuder-Sonnen, "Beyond Integration Theory: The (Anti-)Constitutional Dimension of European Crisis Governance," *Journal of Common Market Studies* 54, no. 6 (2016): 1350 *et seq.*

11. The 795-page compilation *The Key Legal Texts of the European Crises,* by Fernando Losada and Agustín José Menéndez, is available at www.sv.uio.no.

12. D. Innerarity, *Democracy in Europe: A Political Philosophy of the EU* (Cham: Palgrave Macmillan, 2018).

13. Explanatory statement, p. 2.

14. J. Habermas, "European Citizens and European Peoples: The Problem of Transnationalizing Democracy," in *The Lure of Democracy,* p. 29 *et seq.* (Cambridge: Polity Press, 2015).

15. K. Polanyi, *The Great Transformation: The Political and Economic Origins of Our Time* (Boston: Beacon Press, 2001), pp. 253–254 (emphasis in original).

16. ". . . planning was not," ibid., p. 147.

17. F. Block, "Towards a New Understanding of Economic Modernity," in *The Economy as Polity: The Political Construction of Modern Capitalism,* ed. C. Joerges, B. Stråth, and P. Wagner, p. 3 *et seq.* (London: Cavendish, 2005).

18. The democracy notion captures these aspects in similar ways; cf. K. Nicolaidis and M. Watson, "Sharing the Eurocrats' Dream: A Democratic Approach to EMU Governance in the Post-Crisis Era," in *The End of the Eurocrat's Dream,* ed. D. Chalmers, M. Jachtenfuchs, and C. Joerges, p. 50 *et seq.* (Cambridge: Cambridge University Press, 2016); F. Cheneval and F. Schimmelfennig, "The Case for Democracy in the European Union," *Journal of Common Market Studies* 5, no. 1 (2013): 334 *et seq.*

19. W. Abelshauser, *Kulturkampf: Der deutsche Weg in die neue Wirtschaft und die amerikanische Herausforderung* (Berlin: Kadmos, 2003); W. Abelshauser, D. Gilgen, and A. Leutzsch, "Kultur, Wirtschaft, Kulturen der Weltwirtschaft," in *Kulturen der Weltwirtschaft,* ed. W. Abelshauser, D. Gilgen, and A. Leutzsch, p. 9 *et seq.* (Göttingen: Vandenhoek und Ruprecht, 2012); G. Teubner, "Legal

Irritants: Good Faith in British Law or How Unifying Law Ends Up in New Differences," *Modern Law Review* 61 (1998): 11 *et seq.*
20. A. Hassel, "Adjustments in the Eurozone: Varieties of Capitalism and the Crisis in Southern Europe," LEQS Paper no. 76 (2014), http://dx.doi.org/10.2139/ssrn.2436454.
21. Cf. F. W. Scharpf, "After the Crash: A Perspective on Multilevel European Democracy," *European Law Journal* 21, no. 3 (2015): 384 *et seq.*; M. Höpner and A. Schäfer, "A New Phase of European Integration: Organized Capitalisms," *West European Politics* 33, no. 2 (2010): 344 *et seq.*; W. Streeck, "E Pluribus Unum? Varieties and Commonalities of Capitalism," MPIfG Discussion Paper no. 10/12 (2010).
22. Cf., (in)famously, Court of Justice, judgment of December 11, 2007, case C-438/05, *International Transport Workers' Federation, Finnish Seamen's Union v. Viking Line ABP, OÜ Viking Line Eesti* [GC]; Court of Justice, judgment of December 18, 2007, case C-341/05, *Laval un Partneri Ltd v. Svenska Byggnadsarbetareförbundet, Svenska Byggnadsarbetareförbundets avdelning 1, Byggettan und Svenska Elektrikerförbundet* [GC]; Court of Justice, judgment of April 3, 2008, case C-346/06, *Rechtsanwalt Dr. Dirk Rüffert v. Land Niedersachsen.*
23. For an elaboration of this point, see J. Bast, F. Rödl, and J. Terhechte, "Funktionsfähige Tarifvertragssysteme als Grundpfeiler von Binnenmarkt und Währungsunion," *Zeitschrift für Rechtspolitik* 48, no. 8 (2015): 230 *et seq.*
24. See, on these implications and conceivable responses, F. W. Scharpf, "Vom asymmetrischen Euro-Regime in die Transferunion—und was die deutsche Politik dagegen tun könnte," MPIfG Discussion Paper no. 17/15 (2017); Scharpf, "Forced Structural Convergence in the Eurozone," MPIfG Discussion Paper no. 16/15 (2016); Scharpf, "De-Constitutionalization and Majority Rule: A Democratic Vision for Europe," MPIfG Discussion Paper no. 16/14 (201); and most recently, Scharpf, "International Monetary Regimes and the German Model," in MPIfG Discussion Paper no. 18/1 (2018).
25. The T-Dem initiative has recently gained prominent support. In "Sans la création d'un budget européen, Macron ne peut réussir," Harvard political economist Dani Rodrik argued in May 2017 (see https://www.latribune.fr/opinions/tribunes/sans-la-creation-d-un-budget-europeen-macron-ne-peut-reussir-710660.html), and he underlined his agreement with Thomas Piketty's characterization of Macron's "yesterday's Europe" in his *Straight Talk on Trade: Ides for a Sane World Economy* (Princeton: Princeton University Press, 2018), 73, adding: "If European democracies are to regain their health, economic integration and political integration cannot remain out of sync. Either political integration catches up with economic integration or economic integration needs to be scaled back" (76).

13

In Search of Lost Sovereignty

IPHIGÉNIE KAMTSIDOU

Any plan for democratizing the European Union calls to mind the myth of the Danaids, who were condemned by the judges of the Underworld to fill a barrel with a hole in it for all eternity. For the past ten years the democratic deficit that was sapping the legitimacy of European institutions has been doubled: when the banking and financial crisis of 2007–2009 provoked an increase in public debts and deficits, the sole currency was salvaged by establishing a government of the eurozone that reduces the political autonomy of the European peoples and eats away at the foundations of representative democracy.

In effect, the leaders of the European Union and its member states have made recourse to *international public law* and to *soft law* in order to impose a strict budgetary discipline on the states and to require them to administer a heavy dose of austerity to their citizens. The Commission and organs of the eurozone monopolized the power to make decisions of incommensurable weight for European societies, decisions that were independent of every political bond and practically immune to any control. In that way, the precepts of European economic governance were legally overdetermining the political orientation of the Union and its members, thus radicalizing the democratic crisis in Europe.

In order to confront the democratic emergency, the authors of the T-Dem have formulated their plan to democratize Europe by law, taking inspiration from the method employed by the European elites. Concrete and pragmatic, the Treaty's proposal for democratizing the eurozone has the merit of launching debate on possible and necessary reforms of European institutions and, at the same time, highlighting the urgent need to redefine relations between the political and the economic.

An Institutional Architecture Reestablishing Democratic Legitimacy at the European Level

The keystone of the mechanism designed by the T-Dem is the Parliamentary Assembly of the Euro Area, drafted in such a way as to permit the European peoples to reappear on the political scene. In effect, as much by its composition as by its functions, the Parliamentary Assembly is intended to enable citizens to oversee European economic governance and to influence the decision-making processes—in other words, to reconstruct a space in the midst of which questions regarding economic and social policies will be open and susceptible of receiving different answers.

Its democratic vocation rests first of all on the way its members are selected. It is formed of the parliamentarians of the different national parliaments (4/5) and the European Parliament (1/5) in terms of political representation and according to a proportionality applied to the member states. The national parliamentarians, charged with a relatively precise political mandate and being regularly answerable to the voters of their countries, will naturally try to make their national political contract respected in and by the workings of the Assembly. Moreover, their dual membership favors the more active involvement of the parliaments in European procedures: with direct representation in the governing authorities of the eurozone, the national representations will have better knowledge of the stakes and will be able to formulate proposals at the opportune time and, if necessary, apply their veto to policies drafted by the technocrats and the executive. As components of the Assembly, the parliaments will become agents of economic governance—thereby implementing the vision of the Treaty of Lisbon, which seeks to give the parliaments an active role in managing European affairs. Here, the application of the T-Dem shows itself to be an instrument to revitalize the Treaties and a way to integrate the consent of the peoples.

In the tradition of democratic parliamentarism, the Assembly possesses powers to legislate and to control. Now, contrary to what takes place in parliamentary systems, where the balance of the organs and the governing forces is ensured by the supple separation of powers, the T-Dem aims to establish brakes and counterweights through the close collaboration of powers. The legislative process rests on the cooperation of the Eurogroup and the Assembly, who determine its orientation by together setting the legislative agenda, with power granted to the representative body to have priority in submitting proposals or plans, within the limit of one-half of the sessions.

The members of the Assembly hold legislative initiative concurrently with those of the Eurogroup, which gives rise to a rather complex process for adopting legislative acts. In order to initiate a division of sovereignty between the Eurogroup and the Assembly, the T-Dem establishes a legislative shuttle, set up by a committee of conciliation, conceived basically on the model of the mixed joint commission of the French Parliament. In the course of the ordinary legislative process, the committee is convoked to resolve any disagreement between the two organs, and to do that, it has the power to approve a plan for a common text. If it does not succeed in doing so or if its plan is rejected by the Eurogroup or by the Assembly, the latter is called upon to make a definitive ruling.

This structural dialogue can take place for eighteen weeks, during which it will be possible for the organs and their members to discuss, investigate alternatives, and arrive at a consensus. The same modalities are provided by the regulations concerning the budget for the eurozone, within shorter time limits. The T-Dem seems, then, to answer the call, expressed by scholars as well as by political forces and movements, that "a vociferous and argued contest of opinion" frame decision making and determine the choices carried out by the executive, so as to put a stop to the autocratic drift of European governance.

The democratic promise of the T-Dem is sustained by the supervisory missions granted to the Assembly and concerning the European Central Bank and the European Commission, when the latter exercises its task of economic and budgetary coordination and of the fiscal convergence of the member states of the eurozone. It is true that this is far from the situation where the representative body possesses real power of control of the institution that sets monetary policy; the Assembly also does not hold the power to define the budgetary policies that are at the center of European economic governance. But the dialogue envisaged with the ECB, as well as the participation of the Assembly in discussions relative to the proposals of budgetary plans of the member states and to the conditions for implementing the structural reforms recommended for the eurozone, delineates an area where the accountability of the governing parties can develop. Nonetheless, the question arises whether this form of informative communication is able to establish a political bond between the Assembly and the executive and to turn on the democratic current in Europe.

Deficiencies and Constraints: The Lack of Political Responsibility and the Weight of the European Economic Constitution

In fact, one of the original sins that plagues the institutional architecture of the T-Dem is the absence of any mechanism of political responsibility. Concerned to alleviate the defects of parliamentarism and to adapt the institutional mechanism of the Treaty to the characteristics of the supranational structure of the eurozone, the authors of the T-Dem have not provided the Assembly with the power to control the executive politically. As such, neither the Eurogroup nor the Commission is accountable to the representative organ and no political sanction can be imposed on them. Article 11 of the T-Dem is entitled "Powers of Investigation and Control," but its provisions seem to delineate a *quasi-disciplinary* power of the Assembly. Effectively, the only means of control that is established—that is, the possibility of forming a commission of investigation—concerns the bad administration of the "governance of the eurozone" and it is accompanied by the obligation of the Court of Audit of the EU to assist the Assembly in the framework of this task. It is an accommodation that implies that the Assembly is only competent to examine the legality of the Eurogroup's and the Commission's activity and cannot evaluate in political terms their options and their choices.

A motion of censure against the members of the Eurogroup would certainly be inappropriate. The finance ministers who are members of this informal organ serve the political projects of their governments and enjoy the confidence of their countries' parliaments. In the great majority of cases this can put them at a distance from their post. The "doubling up" of their responsibility would thus present itself as either superfluous or hazardous: the change in persons could not influence the policy guidelines decided at the national level, while the sanction inflicted by the Assembly of the Euro Area would constitute formidable mismanagement in the governmental and parliamentarian affairs of the member states: Allowing an international authority—even if it is only representative—to condition the import of the government would further reduce the import of the democratic principle at the national level and would justify reservations about the project.

And yet, this form of parliamentary control regarding the members of the Commission is not inconceivable. The power of the Assembly to examine the activity of the Commissioners in the framework of the exercise of responsibilities having to do with the economic governance of the Union, could be considered the equivalent of censure. The legal obligation of the Commission to resign once the Assembly manifests its rejection, would obligate one of the branches of the European executive to take into consideration the directives formulated by the representatives of the peoples, it would politicize economic policies, and it would acclimatize the democratic play in the Union.

To the dilemma that the workings of the Assembly constitutes for the functioning of the executive, the T-Dem responds by establishing a close collaboration of institutional organs, intended to guarantee the presence of the representative body at the Euro Summits and in the procedures of coordination and convergence. Likewise, the conjunction of the Assembly and the Eurogroup in the exercise of legislative responsibility is the means that preserves the Assembly's power to determine on an equal footing the content of legislative acts and, consequently, to co-define economic policies. Despite the ingenuity of the system, its effectiveness is minimized by a major defect: the risk of the blockage in the case where a disagreement arises between the Assembly and the Eurogroup. In such a case, how is the agenda of the Euro Summit to be set or how is the biannual work schedule of the Eurogroup to be decided? By what method will the Assembly oversee respect for a legislative act it will have adopted at its last reading against the dissent of the Eurogroup? The sin of regimes of rigid separation, where a difference of political orientation between the executive and the parliament leads to inertia, tarnishes the construction of the T-Dem, and merits discussion.

After all, debate on the democratization of the eurozone cannot do without the questions raised by the norms of constitutional order regulating the exercise of responsibilities provided by the T-Dem and delimiting the action of its organs. The T-Dem, in order to satisfy the ambition of supporting the attainment of the objectives of the European Union, provides that it be applied and interpreted in conformity with the Treaties on which the European Union is founded.

Now, the Treaties form the principal part of the "bloc of constitutionality" that for decades has supported the functioning of the European communities and later the Union and that nurtures the democratic deficit in Europe. Constituted under the influence of German ordoliberalism, the Treaties serve to institutionalize economic liberties and rationality, by ensuring the preponderance of the economic Constitution of the Union in relation to the other principles contained either within them or in their common constitutional traditions. In short, despite the enhancement of the primary law by regulations aimed at supporting the constitution of a political community and ameliorating the social statues of its citizens, since the beginning of the twenty-first century a hierarchy has been clearly established—if reestablished—in the European juridical order: with the help of the jurisprudence of the CJEU, the rules that guarantee the protection of dignity and favor democratic participation, are considered as limits, as affronts to communitarian liberties. Consequently, they are subject to a narrow interpretation that substantially delimits their import.

This fundamental hierarchy conditions the power of the Assembly and the Eurogroup, as well as the fate of the legislative provisions they will adopt. The rules whose aim is to favor lasting growth and social cohesion will be examined by the judge in light of the articulation of the principles conveyed by the Treatises; and if they exceed the goals of the economic Constitution, they will be censured. It suffices to consult Article 3 of the TEU, which, while setting as the Union's goal the peace and well-being of its peoples, provides that the social economy of the market should be highly competitive in order to measure the burden of the constraints that will weigh on the Assembly and its work.

Is the public space organized by the T-Dem a sufficient condition to thwart the normative force of the European economic constitution? The experience of the representative democracies in the postmodern era justifies pessimism; but to answer in the negative is to misunderstand the dynamic of a system that preserves the autonomy of political judgment: Because the legislator is the first interpreter of any Constitution, it may be that European citizens will benefit from the institutional mechanism of the T-Dem and provide the Assembly with the opportunity to transform the equilibrium of the fundamental norms and principles governing European policies.

—*Translated by Marc LePain*

14

Reconciling Democratic Sovereignty with Economic and Monetary Integration

T-Dem in Dialogue with the German Constitutional Court

ULRIKE LIEBERT

What relationship is there between the Draft Treaty for Democratizing the Governance of the Euro Area (T-Dem)[1] and the jurisprudence of the German Constitutional Court (GCC)? This is a hypothetical question, unless the eurozone governments adopted the T-Dem and a German opposition party took the German government to the GCC claiming that the T-Dem is anti-constitutional. Only then would the watchdog of Germany's "guarded democracy" scrutinize the legitimacy of this treaty for democratizing the eurozone under the German "Grundgesetz" (Basic Law). Given that the GCC defines its role as that of a "last resort" in exceptional situations,[2] would it judge the T-Dem as a case where "it is for the Federal Republic of Germany due to its responsibility for integration, to work toward a change"? Or, if worst comes to worst, might Germany refuse to further participate in the European Union?[3] But even if the GCC might never rule on the T-Dem, a closer look at the GCC's former jurisprudence on EU treaties is vital for framing the T-Dem for the German normative debate. Through the lenses of the GCC we can identify normative strengths and shortcomings in this original proposal for reform of the Economic and Monetary Union (EMU).

The following puts the T-Dem in dialogue with the GCC to explore critical issues for democratizing the governance of the euro area. I will limit myself to the GCC's 2009 ruling on the Treaty of Lisbon, as this has most extensively laid down the Court's normative presuppositions for the democratic legitimacy of the European Union.[4] I develop this conversation in two parts: In the first part, I ask how the T-Dem positions itself in the German political debate regarding reform of the EMU. In the second part, I examine the T-Dem proposal as to where it fits or risks the GCC's normative requirements for democratic legitimacy beyond the state.

The T-Dem in the Context of the German Debate on EU Reform

In Germany the public debate on the future of Europe has been slow to take off. There has not been an articulate German rejoinder to Jean-Claude Juncker's reform program[5] or Emanuel Macron's vision of a sovereign, united, and democratic EU, let alone to the reform programs of other presidential candidates. Arguably, the contradictory constellation of center-right technocratic conceptions of EMU governance grounded on ideas of "stability" and "market discipline," and center-left proposals for a socially resilient EMU based on "solidarity" and "risk sharing," make it particularly complex to achieve German coalition government and will formation regarding EU reforms.[6]

Yet the German wider public shares the T-Dem's concerns about the populist wave, how to hold in check the threats to European democracies, and how to prevent the dissolution of the European Union. While many would attribute the current malaise to national governments' refusal to jointly govern the mass refugee movement of 2015, the democratic deficits of the EU in general, and its eurozone crisis management in particular, are less salient. Few would deny that the balanced-budget rule has harmed poorer constituencies, regions, and lower middle classes and protected banks and businesses—also in Germany, even if less so than in the southern eurozone countries or France. Nevertheless, ordinary Germans tend to see austerity regimes as a necessary evil and take them for granted. To explain these beliefs, three specificities come to mind: First, due to Germany's exports-led economic success, Germans can be more easily persuaded to accept budget consolidation and debt reduction as preconditions for economic prosperity, rather than to reject them as sources of economic recession, rising unemployment, and socioeconomic inequality. Moreover, in response to the unprecedented centralization of financial and fiscal powers during the eurozone crisis, Germany has strengthened the national parliament vis-à-vis the executive in EU affairs, as an exception to the rule that the eurozone's crisis has undermined democracy in the member states. Also, given the German grand coalition government's unanimous support for the Fiscal Compact and for conditioning financial assistance on hard "adjustment programs" to be implemented by creditor countries, more democratic alternatives to the technocratic paradigm of EMU governance have found only minority support in German political debate, in stark contrast to elsewhere in the eurozone.[7] Over the past decade, German government parties have been eager to place the eurozone in the hands of technocratic agencies and reluctant to democratize it by giving parliamentary politics and national constituents a say.

To the extent to which German discourses on the future of Europe engage a democratic vision for improving the EMU, this is based on a critical analysis of the status quo of governance structures.[8] Although the EU is formally judged to be a democratically legitimate polity, neither member states, including Germany, nor the EU can be qualified as sufficiently democratic in practice. Democratic deficits include lack of transparency (in general in Council procedures and specifically in proceedings of the Euro Summits, the Eurogroup, and the European Stability Mechanism [ESM]), insufficient division of powers, deficient accountability, defective political equality of citizens, and poor participation. In response to these deficits, German political parties from the center to the left put a clear focus on ameliorating the European Parliament (EP). Institutional reforms aim at reinforcing supranational parliamentary legitimacy by buttressing European political parties, institutionalizing the lead-candidate model and the right of the EP to legislative initiative, introducing transnational lists in European elections, and expanding the EP's competences, including a sizable EU budget. There are limits to this approach with regard to legislative powers that the EU under the current Lisbon Treaty does not have but that would be required in order to place the intergovernmental, executive-centered euro-area governance into the Community framework of supranational parliamentary co-decision-making. The caveat of German reform strategies for democratizing the EMU rests on the assumption that a unanimous political will of the EU-27 for fully fledged treaty reforms is unlikely to form in the foreseeable future. Given these constraints, there is increased acceptance of pragmatic ideas for differential integration and for strengthening parliamentary control. This does not necessarily support the creation of a new eurozone parliament, as this threatens to accentuate the divisions between the eurozone and the rest of the EU, and to put at risk the coherence of policies for the single market and the EU. Instead, this is meant to build a eurozone committee within the European Parliament—"more promising and present in the current debate."[9] Moreover, it is proposed to create a joint committee of European and national representatives for joint democratic control of the investment expenditures by the newly created European finance minister and the European Monetary Fund.[10]

Against this background, the T-Dem proposal for creating a new interparliamentary eurozone Assembly should be welcomed as the most far-reaching proposal for a way out of the Eurozone's reform deadlock. Contrary to the right-wing populist "Alternative for Germany" (AfD), interparliamentary cooperation will not be denounced as "unnational," but embraced as a democratic innovation. Not unaccountable agencies but interparliamentary majorities would make choices in full sight of the public. Yet, if the T-Dem promises to unify the eurozone politically, progressives will fear that it might undermine the European Parliament and split the EU into "eurozone-ins" and "eurozone-outs." Conservatives will be worried that it will weaken fiscal responsibility and stability and become very expensive for the EU's net payers (Germany, in particular). Finally, it will be questioned whether the treaty for a democratic eurozone will be able to survive in the shark tank of EU treaty reform, requiring mutually canceling vetoes and potential ratification referenda stirred up by the populists. The T-Dem is designed to shortcut the cumbersome EU Treaty revision procedure by negotiating an international treaty among the eurozone states that will enter into force once ten of them have ratified it. However, is it also designed to ensure approval by the GCC?

The following explores the puzzle of whether the GCC might approve the T-Dem. To what extent is its proposed "democratic transplant into the heart of the existing eurozone system" compatible with the German

Basic Law? The following interpretation draws on the GCC's Lisbon ruling,[11] and aims at identifying points of agreement as well as potential contentions.

Putting the T-Dem in Dialogue with GCC Jurisprudence

To date the GCC has never derailed the process of European integration in cases of EU treaty reform. However, as Joseph Weiler noted, its ruling on the Treaty of Lisbon sounds like a "dog that barks but does not bite": "A decision with lights and shadows, some conflicting tendencies, some painful displays of shallowness and lack of political imagination, and some veritable soaring passages and profound reflection."[12] A case in point for the GCC's enlightening passages is the legal framework it advances for qualifying the sui generis character of the EU as a *Staatenverbund,* or supranational union. This notion differs from established concepts such as *Staatenbund* (confederation of states) or *Bundesstaat* (federal state) insofar as it introduces a new category that presupposes a close and long-term association between sovereign states that exercises the supranational authority of government in the framework of treaties that are available only to the member states and their peoples.[13] Moreover, to characterize the EU as an "association of sovereign states" that are mutually committed to openness, integration, and international law means also to acknowledge the citizens of the member states as the subjects of the EU's democratic legitimacy.[14] In this sense, the 2009 Lisbon Ruling depicts the EU as an "association of democratic peoples" who are the holders of constituent power. In the context of parliamentary democracy under the German Basic Law, this means that legislative bodies need to be accorded sufficient rights of participation in EU decision making.[15] Yet, it will not permit the legislative, executive, or judicial powers to dispose of the essential elements of the constitution, the so-called constitutional identity (art. 23.1, sentence 3, art. 79.3 GG), without having the popular sovereign give its consent. Finally, in depicting German constitutional identity, the GCC underscores its the principle of *Europarechtsfreundlichkeit* (European-law friendliness), to which the Basic Law is committed and which requires all constitutional powers of the Federal Republic of Germany to "participate in the development of a democratic, social and federal European Union."[16]

Drawing on this conceptual framework, I will explore the relationship between GCC jurisprudence and the T-Dem more in detail, along six key topics.

I. Starting with points of agreement, the GCC as well as the T-Dem take popular sovereignty and democracy seriously, as they share the aim of reconciling European integration with the sovereignties of the democratic peoples. More specifically, the GCC has conditioned the further deepening of European integration on the "principle of democracy." This "fundamental right for a democratically elected representative who has still something to decide"[17] affirms the "continuing sovereignty of the member states' people . . . anchored in the Member States"[18] and is "contained in the last instance in the German Constitution."[19] The GCC further acknowledges the "sui-generis nature" of the EU, depicting it as a "system of federal and supranational intertwining of power."[20] It concludes that "the democracy of the European Union cannot, and need not, be shaped in analogy to that of a state. Instead, the European Union is free to look for its own ways of democratic supplementation by means of additional, novel forms of transparent or participative political decision-making."[21] The GCC therefore supports also elements of "associative and direct democracy"—that is, citizens' consultation and participation, according to "the precept of providing, in a suitable manner, the citizens of the Union and 'representative' associations with the possibility of making their views heard in the EU." Obviously, the T-Dem draws on the general normative framework by conditioning its proposal for EMU reform on the "principle of democracy," albeit limited to institutional forms of representative parliamentary governance.

II. As regards the institutional forms to embody the democratic principle for European integration, the GCC has mostly stressed what does not work rather than what works. On the one hand, it observes that the Lisbon Treaty changes the EP's composition so that it will no longer consist of "representatives of the people of the States brought together in the Community" but instead will consist of "representatives of the 'Union's citizens.'"[22] It further acknowledges that "the citizens of the Union are granted a right to participate in the democratic life of the Union (Article 10.3, Article 11.1 TEU Lisbon), which emphasizes a necessary structural connection between the civic polity and public authority."[23] On the other hand, it also identifies a caveat that detracts from the EP's potential for democratic legitimation. In the GCC's view,

the current configuration of the EP does not live up to normative requirements,[24] because it negates European citizens' status as legitimating
subjects[25] as long as voting rules do not comply with "the democratic
precept of electoral equality" in the Council and in the EP.[26] It is a major
strength of the T-Dem's design of the eurozone parliament that it avoids
this pitfall. First, rather than pave the way toward a supranational legislative state branch, it seeks to institutionalize a transnational Assembly
that is designed to draw from among the members of national parliaments in proportion to the size of their countries' populations. This provision would do justice to the norm established by the GCC that democratic
legitimation by a representative assembly requires electoral equality.
Yet, increasing the proportion of seats for larger member states as compared to smaller ones is only one normative requirement for resolving
deficits of democratic legitimacy of the eurozone's parliamentary governance, as the GCC elaborates on further preconditions.

III. In addition, the GCC has underscored that a democratically legitimate European parliament would presuppose European public debate and open expression of opinion. For the Lisbon ruling, democratic
legitimization goes beyond electoral democracy—it requires also at the
domestic level a viable public sphere: "Democracy first and foremost,
lives on, and in, a viable public opinion that concentrates on central acts
of determination of political direction and the periodic allocation of
highest-ranking political offices in the competition. . . . Only this public
opinion makes visible the alternatives for elections and other votes."[27]
The fact that European citizens and mass media show little interest in
the European Parliament's debates is generally attributed to the per-
ception that the EP's powers are too weak, especially in areas of direct
importance to citizens such as social policy, and in particular lack the
right to legislative initiative. Under the T-Dem, the new transnational
Parliamentary Assembly would draw on the representatives and powers
hitherto in the hands of the national parliaments of the eurozone. It
can be expected to draw citizens' attention and interest at the same time
on the same issues in all member states, as it will have the authority
to decide in the areas of budgetary, fiscal, social, and economic policy,
all of which have a direct impact on eurozone citizens' lives.[28] Under the
T-Dem a considerably augmented budget is supposed to empower the
eurozone parliament as it will be able to choose among substantive policy
alternatives—for instance, regarding sustainable growth, employment,

social cohesion, and economic and financial convergence in the euro-zone. However, the eurozone Assembly would strengthen the eurozone's democratic legitimacy only to the extent that it succeeds in mediating among national and supranational conflicts of interests and identities to jointly exercise the powers of program planning, oversight, investigation, and decision making.

IV. Moreover, an interpretation of the T-Dem from the GCC's sovereignist angle offers strong support in favor of a European legal order—conceived by an international treaty, based on "delegated authority," and premised on national sovereignty—that links the authority of the EU to the "principle of conferral," which is a "mechanism of protection to preserve the Member States' responsibility."[29] In its Lisbon Ruling, the GCC erects the Basic Law as an "integration barrier" against constitution-building aimed at an EU state.[30] Therefore, the GCC exhibits a clear sympathy for an international treaty rather than a European constitution, in line with the notion that the states are to remain the EU's "masters of the treaties."[31] This is clearly an area of understanding with the T-Dem recommending—albeit for pragmatic reasons—an international treaty to be concluded by the eurozone governments, therefore building on two precedents, both accepted by the GCC: the Fiscal Compact and the ESM. However, potential tensions with the GCC may arise for the T-Dem because it differs from previous eurozone treaties on a sensitive issue: It replaces unanimity as the decision-rule among finance ministers in the Eurogroup and heads of state and government in the Euro Summit by the majority rule as the ordinary legislative procedure in the eurozone. This means that the T-Dem is positioned to depart from the ESM, which protects the veto power of the big creditor states—which, under the T-Dem, will no longer have their current de facto veto power in inter-state proceedings.

V. Regarding its red lines, the CGG has warned against treaty changes aimed at transforming the EU into a supranational democratic federal state. In the court's interpretation, the Treaty of Lisbon introduces elements of supranational statehood:[32] From state symbols that are recognized by a large number of member states, to the widening of Council majority decision-making, and to European Parliamentary co-decision-making becoming the rule, the institutional setup of the Union becomes more state-like than before. Furthermore, although "citizenship of the Union" is conceived as "additional to national citizenship" (art. 8), citizens are acknowledged as being "directly represented at Union level in the European Parliament" and, thus, as the constituency of the latter (art. 8A, 2). Moreover, the preamble of the Treaty as well as the Charter of Fundamental Rights outline the values on which the constitutional order of the EU rests. Finally, although the Lisbon Treaty does not establish the principle of primacy of EU law, it includes a "Declaration concerning Primacy" that describes the primacy of EU law as a matter of fact, or by convention.[33] Different from a transformation of the EU into a federal democratic state, the T-Dem would not require constitutional revisions of the German Basic Law. With the GCC it is ready to acknowledge the existence of a functional constitution at the Union level[34] as well as the primacy of EU law over national primary law. This not withstanding, the T-Dem steps into the risky territory of a state-like development: "To the extent that the development of the European Union in analogy to a state would be continued on the basis of the Treaty of Lisbon, which is open to development in this context, this would be in contradiction to constitutional foundations. Such a step, however, has not been made by the Treaty of Lisbon."[35] On the question whether it moves the eurozone toward statehood, the T-Dem remains silent. This could be a point of weakness, as the eurozone Assembly is designed to take over resources and powers that could detract from the core of national constitutional identity under the Basic Law.

VI. Finally, it remains an open question whether the GCC would be ready to endorse transnational modes of parliamentary democracy that constitute a political union: "Political union means the joint exercise of public authority, including the legislative authority, which even reaches into the traditional core areas of the state's area of competence."[36] However, in the next paragraph the Lisbon Ruling defines the scope of material areas that member states need for retaining "sufficient space for the political formation of the economic, cultural and social circumstances of life": namely, state citizenship, state monopoly of violence, fiscal decisions, criminal law, culture and education, freedom of opinion, press, assembly, and religion, and social welfare.[37] Any EU reform that would decouple the core principle of popular democratic legitimacy from the national context and transfer it to the transnational or even supranational realm would be judged against this normative framework. If a treaty moved beyond the fine lines between both elaborated by the judges, it would infringe with Germany's democratic core identity. The only way out left then would be a historical novelty for post-WWII Germany—a federal referendum. The GCC's insistence on high thresholds for a European democratic federal state is not necessarily reluctance tout court, but should be read as the claim that a "Constitutional moment" and the revision of the Basic Law are required at the threshold from the status quo of a confederal union to "supranational statehood." The crucial question is whether the proposed T-Dem interferes with these red lines—or, alternatively, escapes this dichotomy and manages to get around the alleged gulf between national versus supranational democratic statehood.

Conclusions

Putting the T-Dem in dialogue with the German Constitutional Court sheds light on the tricky issues of how to reconcile democratic sovereignty with economic and monetary integration. Karlsruhe can be commended for placing the democratic deficits of European integration at center stage, for protecting the German constitutional identity against "excessive federalization," and, moreover, for calling on the Bundestag and Bundesrat to effectively assume their democratic "Integrationsverantwortung" (responsibility in EU integration matters). All the same, in relation to the T-Dem the GCC can hardly be said to offer a coherent, clear-cut model for what, arguably, should and could be a framework for European democracy. While cherishing national democratic sovereignty in a Union of states, the Lisbon Ruling acknowledges the evolving practices of transnational, multilateral, and multilevel governance. It also clarifies which preconditions for democratic legitimacy the judges expect a "Federal Republic of Europe"[38] to meet. Arguably, this device cannot be generalized to inform the agenda for democratic reforms of the eurozone, let alone the EU, unless the GCC is ready to revise its dichotomous construction of national popular sovereignty versus supranational statehood.

The argument developed here is that the T-Dem conveys a coherent message about a democratically appropriate order of euro-area governance, and that this resonates with the constitutional debate in Germany. In the context of the German political debate, the T-Dem is superior to other proposals that have been aired in so far, as it takes into account the multilevel structure of government in the EU. The eurozone parliament would bundle the sovereignties of both national and European levels. A eurozone legislature created in this manner would no longer have reason to fear the present political preeminence of the executive and legislative branches. Also tipping the scales in its favor would be the enhanced capacity of the eurozone to get important tasks accomplished, especially channeling global financial flows and shaping the economic and monetary order in Europe. Nevertheless, this institutional framework will not work without a narrative that addresses the concerns voiced by advocates of EU cohesion and democratization through strengthening European elections and the European Parliament. To build support among German publics for moving ahead into the next stage of democratization, the most sensitive issue are efforts to strengthen the eurozone's parliamentary politics in modes that do not risk lasting splits in the EU and the single market. Rescuing the euro and keeping the European Union together will only work if the countries not yet in the eurozone will be kept on the towline or even to want to come on board.

Notes

1. The draft treaty proposal by Stephanie Hennette, Thomas Piketty, Guillaume Sacriste, and Antoine Vauchez was developed for the French 2017 presidential election campaign and originally published in book form under the title *Pour un traité de democratization de l'Europe* (Seuil, 2017).
2. GCC, ¶¶240, 245.
3. GCC, ¶264.
4. The Treaty of Lisbon amending the Treaty on European Union and the Treaty establishing the European Community, was signed at Lisbon, December 13, 2007 (2007 / C 306 / 01), Official Journal of the European Union C 306, title II., art. 8 A, B and C. It establishes a new title with provisions on democratic principles for the activities and functions of the Union, including citizens' equality, representative democracy, participatory and consultation mechanisms, such as the citizens' legislative initiative, and the role of national parliaments.
5. Jean-Claude Juncker, "State of the European Union" (European Parliament, Strasbourg, September 13, 2017).
6. For a recent technocratic proposal, see Johannes Becker and Clemens Fuest, *Der Odysseus Komplex: Ein pragmatischer Vorschlag zur Lösung der Eurokrise* (Hanser, 2017); for a "progressive perspective from Germany," see Alexander Schellinger and Philipp Steinberg, eds., *The Future of the Eurozone: How to Keep*

Europe Together (transcript, 2017). A most recent attempt to reconcile these contrasting paradigms can be found in the report "Reconciling Risk Sharing with Market Discipline: A Constructive Approach to Euro Area Reform," CEPR Policy Insight Paper no. 91 (2018), by a French-German group of economists including Henrik Enderlein, Marcel Fratzscher, Clemens Fuest, Jean Pisani-Ferry, Isabel Schnabel, Betrice Weder di Mauro and others.

7. See Ulrike Liebert: "'TINA' Revisited: Why Alternative Narratives of the Eurozone Crisis Matter," in *After the Financial Crisis: Shifting Legal, Economic and Political Paradigms*, ed. Pablo Iglesias-Rodríguez, Anna Triandafyllidou, and Ruby Gropas, 303–334 (Palgrave, 2016).

8. See Daniela Schwarzer, "An Institutional Framework for the Reformed Eurozone," in Schellinger and Steinberg, *The Future of the Eurozone.*

9. Ibid., 68.

10. See Henrik Enderlein and Jörg Haas, "Was würde ein Europäischer Finanzminister tun? Ein Vorschlag," Policy Paper 145, Jacques Delors Institute (2015).

11. For the Lisbon ruling of the German Constitutional Court, see BVerfG, 2 BvE 2/08 vom 30.6.2009, Absatz-Nr. (1-421), http://www.bverfg.de /entscheidungen/es20090630_2bve000208en.html.

12. Joseph H. Weiler, "Editorial: The 'Lisbon Urteil' and the Fast Food Culture," *European Journal of International Law* 20, no. 3 (October 22, 2009), http://www .ejil.org/pdfs/20/3/1857.pdf .

13. See *Gabler Wirtschaftslexikon, Stichwort: Staatenverbund* (Springer Gabler Verlag), http://wirtschaftslexikon.gabler.de/Archiv/15211/staatenverbund -v9.html.

14. GCC, para. 229.

15. http://www.bundesverfassungsgericht.de/en/press/bvg09-072en.html.

16. The German Basic Law, art. 23 [European Union—Protection of Basic Rights—Principle of Subsidiarity] establishes: "(1) With a view to establishing a united Europe, the Federal Republic of Germany shall participate in the development of the European Union that is committed to democratic, social, and federal principles, to the rule of law, and to the principle of subsidiarity, and that guarantees a level of protection of basic rights essentially comparable to that afforded by this Basic Law. To this end the Federation may transfer sovereign powers by a law with the consent of the Bundesrat."

17. GCC, ¶¶178, 181.

18. GCC, ¶334.

19. GCC, ¶340.

20. GCC, ¶246.

21. GCC, ¶272.

22. GCC, ¶42.

23. GCC, ¶348.

24. GCC, ¶¶271, 276, 295.

25. GCC, ¶347.

26. GCC, ¶¶292, 294.
27. GCC, ¶250.
28. Ulrike Liebert and Hans-Jörg Trenz, "Between Norms and Practices of the Public Sphere: Assessing the Infrastructures for Democracy in Europe," in Erik O. Eriksen and John Erik Fossum, eds., *Reconstituting Democracy in Europe—Theory in Practice,* RECON Report No. 8, ARENA Report 2/09, Oslo (September 2009), 163–196. Available online at: http://www.reconproject.eu/projectweb/portalproject/Report8_TheoryInPractice.html.
29. GCC, ¶301.
30. Dieter Grimm, "Das Grundgesetz als Riegel vor einer Verstaatlichung der Europäischen Union," *Der Staat* (April 2009).
31. GCC, ¶334.
32. Normatively speaking, a democratic European federal state would be expected to rest on (a) a unitary and state-like entity at the Union level similar to democratic states at the national level; (b) a notion of democratic legitimacy of the multilevel EU polity that is rooted primarily in the constituencies of the supranational institutions and secondarily in those of the member states; (c) a European constitutional democratic order based on shared cultural and social norms that serve to avoid or regulate conflict; (d) a process of European constitution-building where EU law enjoys primacy over national constitutional laws that are required to change in order to adapt to EU primary law; see Erik O. Eriksen and John E. Fossum, "Europe's Challenge: Reconstituting Europe or Reconstituting Democracy," in Eriksen and Fossum, *Reconstituting Democracy in Europe—Theory in Practice.*
33. GCC, ¶264.
34. GCC, ¶231.
35. GCC, ¶376.
36. GCC, ¶248.
37. GCC, ¶249.
38. See Stefan Collignon, *Bundesrepublik Europa? Die demokratische Herausforderung und Europas Krise* (Berlin, 2008).

15

Citizen-Based Paths of Democratization for the EU without New Treaty Making

RUI TAVARES

Defending the creation of an EU-wide democracy is a thankless mission. Superficially, it may seem that both euroskeptics and pro-Europeans believe that—whatever your other opinions about the European project—while the European Union exists, it needs to be more democratic. Scratch below the surface, however, and you will find an unholy alliance between a subset of both the pro-Europeans and the euroskeptics intent on keeping at bay the *threat*—not the opportunity—of EU democracy. For pro-Europeans of a certain bureaucratic or intergovernmental bent, the main problem with the EU is not that it is not democratic enough, but that it is not effective enough—and more democracy, in their view, may even obstruct the *output legitimacy* of the EU at the price of an elusive *input legitimacy*. For the more cynical euroskeptics, their opposition was never really to a lack of European democracy but to European integration itself—which entails opposition to any kind of proposal that would make European integration more legitimate. The practical end result of both these positions is the maintenance of the status quo, which is of service to the institutionalized pro-Europeans in strategic terms and to the political euroskeptics in tactical terms.

To counter the obstacle that this unholy alliance poses to the democratization of the EU, defenders of European democracy must achieve a difficult political feat. First, they must create convergences between tribes that seldom agree to work hand-in-hand in the daily reality of European politics.[1] These alliances would have to encompass disillusioned pro-Europeans, the small but active crowd of European federalists, and even euroskeptics in the strict sense (people who doubt the European project but would support the EU if it was proven that it could work both effectively and democratically). In order to do that, EU-democratizers need to work on practical proposals imaginative enough to pierce the wall of indifference to the complexities of EU policy, broad enough to appeal to the linguistically and politically fragmented European polity, and realistic enough to be able to shift the debate from the question of "why the EU cannot work" to the question of how the EU could be made to work better and be more responsive to the people.

The proposal for a Treaty for the Democratization of the Governance of the Euro Area, nicknamed "T-Dem" by its authors Stéphanie Hennette, Thomas Piketty, Guillaume Sacriste and Antoine Vauchez, gets this balance right. The idea that the eurozone can be democratized, via the creation of a Eurozone Assembly, is imaginative enough to catch the attention of those who have been alarmed by the effects of the acute crisis in the EU's single currency. Its appeal is broad enough to interest the public opinions of both indebted and surplus countries, which have been pitted against one another by the structural problems of the euro. And its authors have gone to great lengths to address the question of how to implement the idea of the Eurozone Assembly via a new international treaty, whose first draft they have already set in sound juridical basis. For all of this alone they should be highly commended.

One can, of course, find faults with the actual contents of the T-Dem. Some of them will be on matters of

(a) constitutional importance—Wouldn't the creation of a Eurozone Assembly erode in practice the standing (if not, as the authors claim, the competences) of the European Parliament and thus preempt it from fulfilling its EU legislator role in matters regarding the EU single currency?

(b) practical feasibility—Would smaller EU member states really agree to a smaller version of the Eurozone Assembly where their parliaments would be represented by less than a handful of deputies, which in turn would make it impossible for them to represent their political diversity in the newly established Assembly?

(c) matters of taste—Wouldn't a bigger Eurozone Assembly, decided in order to address the last objection, probably be unpalatable to a *demos* that is sick and tired of outsized institutions, with their privileges, protocols, and budgets to fit?

As soon as you miss the correct balance, the unholy alliance I described in the beginning will just need to tip the scales of the debate in order to kill off yet another well-meaning EU democratization proposal.[2] In the famous words of Lampedusa's *Gattopardo,* under a situation of popular demand for change "some things have to change in order for everything to stay the same." In the rarefied state of EU policy making, it is the other way around: in order for everything to stay the same, you do not have to show that things work well today, but simply find a weak point in any new proposal where just enough political pressure has to be applied for a crucial set of deciders to believe that the changes in view are not worth the effort. In this case, the crucial set of deciders happens to be the EU member state governments.

In the type of situation that I am alluding to, the main strength of the T-Dem proposal may perhaps become one its main weaknesses: because the T-Dem would be firmly grounded on a new international treaty outside of the EU framework, it would seem vulnerable to the notion that an international treaty cannot be valid without being signed by the interested parties—in this case, the EU or eurozone governments. The authors correctly point out, though, that this has already happened—twice. In late 2011, not only the eurozone member states but almost all EU member states (with the exception of the UK and the Czech Republic) signed two treaties outside of the EU treaty framework in order (1) to establish the European Stability Mechanism, which provides a backstop fund for euro countries facing the threat of default, and (2) to set common fiscal and budgetary targets (the "Fiscal Compact"), without which member states would be left without access to that backstop fund.[3] If this was done twice, why not three times? The answer, very simply, is (and was): money. By the end of 2011, indebted countries needed the money; creditor countries would only provide the money if their worries about the debtors' long-term commitment to diminishing their deficits and public debts were assuaged. In those conditions, it is always much easier to sign a contract—or an international treaty—than when one is not in a state of political duress. Unfortunately, the need for deep democratic reforms in eurozone governance is never as pressing for national governments as the need to keep public debt interest rates low; creditor states (including their parliaments, such as the Bundestag, which gained a greater say during the crisis by exerting threats of non-approval for the successive bailout tranches) would lose the most in terms of balance of power if such a reform went through, which makes it doubtful that they would be willing to offer financial stability against a democratization of the euro.

Of course, political conditions may change again in a way that would create a window of opportunity similar to the one of 2011 but with an opposite direction of travel. For that, a crisis would have to arise that would be impossible to solve without the cooperation of a group of member states already politically committed to make any such solution dependent on the acceptance of a T-Dem for the eurozone. This is a circumstance that could (and should) be anticipated through political concertation in intra-EU groupings and summits such as the Euro Med7 Group (Cyprus, France, Greece, Italy, Malta, Portugal, and Spain). But that leaves behind one important question: Apart from creating the preparatory political conditions for member states to accept the drafting a new international treaty between EU or euro states (or to amend the existing EU treaties), is there nothing that can be done before a crisis occurs with all the correct features needed for a democratic pressure to be successful at that point?

Or, to go back to the Beckettian flavor of my title: Given that the arrival of an intergovernmental predisposition for European democracy may prove to be ever-elusive, is there nothing one can do *while we are waiting for a T-Dem?*

Some proposals for a more democratic eurozone governance, compatible with the T-Dem goals and ideals, have already been advanced. The problem at hand is that with the centrality of the single currency and its crisis, the Eurogroup has gained executive-like powers without the equivalent formal mechanisms of legitimacy and oversight that would be essential to control and legitimize those powers. The Eurogroup president, for instance, is not under obligation to respond to the European Parliament and—not being an EU institution *per se*—also does not have clear obligations regarding the Charter of Fundamental Rights of the EU. The idea of a full-time Eurogroup president or a even a "euro-area finance minister," who could—as is the case of the EU's

High Representative for External Affairs—be a member of both the Council of the EU and the European Commission, and thus be accountable to the European Parliament (and also under the purview of the Court of Justice of the EU, with an obligation to obey to the EU Charter of Fundamental Rights), has been advanced by many EU political actors, including in a European Parliament own-initiative report.[4] The same for the possibility of creating a European Parliament super-committee on the euro, which could have greater powers of scrutiny over the appointment of the European Central Bank president.

In order to fulfil the conditions that I have set out in the beginning, any further recommendations must be (1) imaginative enough to pierce the wall of indifference toward EU policy (or perplexity regarding its complexity); (2) realistic, now with the added stricture of being feasible without treaty change or the drafting of new treaties; and (3) broad enough to gather support from, and possibly create political majorities with, different EU constituencies or "tribes."

Of these three conditions, the last one seems to me the most difficult. To start with, it is very difficult to enunciate proposals that would satisfy the requirements of EU integrationists and what we could call "national devolutionists." To be practical in the immediate political conditions, a democratic proposal that could count on the support of both constituencies, or at least not guarantee the rabid opposition of one, or even maybe both, must escape the "more Europe" versus "more nation-state" political dilemma.

One first proposal should deal with the democratization of the Council. In fact, that's also the T-Dem's goal: behind the need to democratize eurozone governance lies the opacity and "informality" of the Eurogroup decision-making process. And behind the Eurogroup and its defects lies the illegibility of the most complex and least understood EU institution: the Council. The Eurogroup is, after all, a "formation" of the Council of the EU, albeit an informal one, and its deliberations feed into the formal decisions of another Council formation, the Economic and Financial Affairs Council (ECOFIN) meeting of EU ministers of finance.

The Council is a two-headed creature. Its first avatar is the European Council, well known for its summits of EU chiefs of state and government, and defined by the treaties as a political priority-setting institution. Then there is the Council of the EU, which shares its staff and headquarters with the European Council, and whose function is to serve as a legislative institution of the EU, along with the European Parliament. The Council of the EU meets in a series of thematic "formations" that can have formal legislative powers (in the case of economic and financial governance, the ECOFIN) or informal agenda-setting powers (the Eurogroup). Less well known, however, is that the day-to-day business of the Council is run by coordination meetings of ambassadors, two per member state, known by their acronyms COREPER 1 and 2 (for Conseil des Representants Permanents).[5] In many meetings where cabinet ministers are not present, it is for the diplomats to cast the votes of their respective countries; even when ministers are present, most of the decisions before their formal meeting would have been deliberated among the diplomatic corps (the several REPER—Répresentations Permanentes) in Brussels. While this mechanism is common in many international organizations, it is clearly outdated when due consideration is given to the level of integration in the EU—let alone the eurozone—and the scope of the legislative decisions that are taken by the Council. The fact that legislative decisions are taken by ambassadors is a—largely unknown to the wider public—remnant of the time when European politics was foreign affairs. Those days are now long gone: for many EU and particularly eurozone countries, European politics is just another aspect of their domestic politics, and a co-legislator of the EU should no longer be run as a diplomatic negotiation forum but be composed of legislators elected either directly or via national parliaments.

As the European Parliament has also evolved from a parliamentary assembly (typical of international organizations such as NATO and the Council of Europe) to a directly elected co-legislator, so should the Council of the EU evolve into something closer to a democratically elected second chamber in all its aspects. One way to do it—entirely consistent, in my view, with the desiderata of the T-Dem—would be to elect the Permanent Representatives through the national parliaments of EU and eurozone member states. This would "senatorialize" the Council in a way similar to the nineteenth-century US Congress. Crucially, this can be done via national legislative decisions, without the need for new treaties or treaty amendments. Some individual member states could take the decision to directly elect the Permanent Representatives, thus legitimating their own democratically elected "senators" to the high chamber of the EU.[6] These elected Permanent Representatives

would answer before their national parliaments and be more accountable to the European public in matters of legislation—thus politicizing
the EU and eurozone legislative procedures in a way that would satisfy
the demands of both the integrationists and the devolutionists. This
would be a democratic reform that would mean "more Europe" and
"more national control" at the same time. Furthermore, the Permanent
Representatives—two per member state, with the differences in voting
rights already stipulated by the EU treaties—could participate in joint
meetings with the European Parliament's super-committee on eurozone
affairs—a joint meeting that would be similar to the Eurozone Congress
structure proposed by Luuk van Midelaar and Vestert Borger in Chapter 11
of this volume.

A greater catalyzer effect could be achieved if several EU or eurozone countries would advance jointly toward a democratic reform of
their permanent representations in the Council of the EU. This could be
done via a "reinforced cooperation" mechanism, which could include
other goals to be advanced by their chamber of parliamentarily or democratically legitimized "senators." The creation of sectoral and regional
agencies in order to deal with the economic and social consequences of
asymmetric shocks inside the eurozone—in effect, complementing the
stabilizing goal of the European Stability Mechanism—could be envisaged. I have elsewhere suggested that the eurozone should have a cross-
disciplinary "Ulysses Agency" dedicated to the multifaceted policies of
stability and growth in crisis-afflicted areas. Such an agency could be
the locus of increased democratic innovation and parliamentary cooperation of the type foreseen by the T-Dem authors.

Lastly, one should not forget that the challenges for democracy in
Europe presently go much beyond the issues of economic governance in
the eurozone area. The values of the EU itself—democracy, rule of law,
respect for human rights—are at risk in the so-called illiberal democracies inside the EU bloc but, for the moment, outside the eurozone. Although outside the remit of this volume, this is where an even more
ambitious T-Dem needs to come to the help of the European Project.
These problems could be addressed through the creation of an EU
Democratic Charter, to be discussed by the European Parliament and
proposed by the eurozone member states as an additional political condition to the entry in the eurozone. In this way the euro could be once
again assumed as what it was supposed to be from the beginning—not

merely a currency, but the spearhead of "ever closer union" and the up-holding of the European promise of democracy, fundamental rights, and shared prosperity in the continent.

Democratizing and "senatorializing" the Council of the EU; creating a Ulysses Agency dedicated to recovery policies in regions afflicted by asymmetric shocks inside the eurozone; and drafting a Democratic Charter of the EU that would reinforce the values of the European project against its illiberal challengers. These would be three democratic and social reforms that could be advanced "while we are waiting for a T-Dem" and entirely consistent, in my view, with the T-Dem's goals and ideals.

Notes

1. Cf. Thomas Raines, Matthew Goodwin, and David Cutts, "Europe's Political Tribes: Exploring the Diversity of Views across the EU," Chatham House (2017), https://www.chathamhouse.org/sites/files/chathamhouse/publi cations/research/2017-12-01-europes-political-tribes-raines-goodwin -cutts.pdf.
2. As these words were being written, the defeat of the proposal to create a pan-European constituency with transnational voting lists for the European Parliament elections, at the hands of both the most powerful "pro-European" party, the EPP, and the euroskeptic parliamentarians from both the far right and the radical left, has provided a very accurate illustration of the kind of obstacle I try to describe here (cf. Motion for a Resolution, *Composition of the European Parliament*, February 7, 2018, http://www.votewatch.eu/en/term8 -composition-of-the-european-parliament-motion-for-resolution-vote -resolution-as-a-whole.html).
3. In its famous *Pringle* case, the Court of Justice of the EU judged that this methodology was not incompatible with the EU treaties.
4. Elmar Brok and Mercedes Bresso, European Parliament Report on Im-proving the Functioning of the European Union, February 2017.
5. Confusingly, COREPER 2 is usually the chief of mission and COREPER 1 their second-in-line.
6. In the United States of America, the State of Oregon first decided to have directly elected senators in 1913, soon to be followed by many other US states, *before* a constitutional amendment.

PART FOUR

REJOINDERS

The T-Dem: Why? How?

Must the idea of reforming Europe be given up? Is it possible to get out of the destructive dilemma between either EU economic policies in which social expectations and political demands never manage to make a way for themselves, or a defensive national game where the only politics concerns the power balance between "the national" and the "the European"? The proposed Treaty on the Democratization of the Governance of the Euro Area (T-Dem), which has been composed jointly by an economist, a legal expert, and two political scientists, sets out the institutional underpinning for a new political compromise capable of opening up genuine alternatives at the core of the European project.[1]

Why seek to "democratize" the governance of the euro area? Is it that the heads of state and government are not themselves democratically responsible?

A new government has come into being in Europe and gained autonomy amid the emergency of the sovereign debt crisis. It comprises the Eurogroup (council of finance ministers) and the Euro Summits (meetings of heads of state and government), but also the Commission, the European Central Bank, and the European Stability Mechanism. In the name of saving the euro, this network of (national and EU) economic bureaucracies has acquired important powers to oversee and monitor *national* economic and budgetary policies. And it has also become the locus for defining the political agenda and watchwords of national "reform" (austerity policies, competitiveness, structural labor market reforms, and so on).

This level of government power, which has more and more budgetary, fiscal, and social ramifications, is today marked by a steep technocratic incline. Its deliberations and decisions completely elude democratic political control: they are taken by opaque, "extraordinary" institutions not provided for in any text, which do not have to account for themselves either to the (sidelined) European Parliament or to national parliaments (which can at most keep tabs on their own government, on the rare occasions when they do even that). Pierre Moscovici, one of the people most familiar with the Eurogroup, recently recognized that it cannot be left "to take its own decisions, to decide on budgetary policy (of the eurozone states) or the future of Greece, for example, late at night behind closed doors."

Why should we think that a change in the balance of powers will change European economic policies?

To introduce a Parliamentary Assembly at the heart of this new power bloc, as the T-Dem proposes, is not simply an institutional question of the balance of powers. In fact, there is a strong link between the form of this new European power (opaque, unaccountable) and the very content of the economic policies (deaf to the social expectations of EU citizens) that it conducts. For this network of bureaucracies and political leaders is currently marked by a strong dynamic of *internal integration,* as a result of which it is becoming more and more *distant* from the political and social "demands" coming from the players in national political spaces. This produces a kind of *deafness* to the expectations expressed by voters and those they elect; it also produces a kind of immunization against the alarm signals coming from the international community of economists (for example, with regard to the economic effectiveness of austerity policies) as well as from NGOs or European institutions concerned with economic and social rights (regarding the social situation in Greece, for instance).

By means of its proposed democratic transplant, the T-Dem aims to open up a space that will make audible other expectations and other social interests than those currently taken into consideration in the factory of European economic policies. It offers the means to develop *concrete* political campaigns (gearing the EU budget to investment, combating of tax fraud, pooling of debts, and so forth), which are alone capable of establishing new social alliances to pull the "European project" away from its technocratic incline.

Is it possible to act quickly? (And, if so, how?)

Yes, it is possible—so long as we give up, in a short period of time, the idea of one "big night" that will institutionally remold the whole of the European Union (the 27 member states). That is not only very unlikely; it is probably not even desirable today, given the coalitions in power in Poland and Hungary. But there is another way: the eurozone leaders themselves have opened it up over the past decade, for better or for worse. When it was a question of restoring the confidence of financial markets in the euro, they knew how to act fast and find the means to construct new policies among the 19 member states of the eurozone. And they did this without a general revision of the treaties signed by all 27 member states. They did it twice, in 2011 and 2012, with the Treaty Establishing the European Stability Mechanism and the Treaty on Stability, Coordination and Governance.

The T-Dem rushes forward onto this path: it uses the large room for maneuver that was discovered in tackling the financial emergency, but this time it employs it to tackle the democratic emergency and to make possible the creation of a eurozone Parliamentary Assembly. This legal avenue could work tomorrow if 10 eurozone states, representing 70% of the population, were to ratify the treaty.

Such immediate feasibility has a trade-off, however. Action by members of the eurozone cannot touch the "Europe of 27," which can be changed only by the 27! Hence, the T-Dem cannot be thought of as a blank slate: while it is possible to find major room for maneuver to drive change forward, the need to respect the "Europe of 27" as it exists today affects the cleanness of the lines. But that is not the main point; the innovations in the T-Dem go sufficiently deep (creation of a Parliamentary Assembly to oversee the governance of the euro area, a euro-area budget funded out of corporate taxation, the pooling of national public debts above 60% of GDP, and so on) to enable a profound reorientation of European construction. All this would actually change the face of Europe.

So, you propose a new Parliamentary Assembly as a counter-weight to the government of the euro area. Would it not be much simpler just to have a Eurozone Commission of the 19 within the European Parliament of the 27?

The idea has the merit of simplicity, but it would be a false step because it completely bypasses the critical issue in the present phase of European integration. Europe has changed profoundly over the past ten years. As was made clear by the heavy adjustment policies imposed on a series of member states (Cyprus, Greece, Ireland, Portugal, Spain) by the Euro-group since 2012, the classical decoupling of what concerns "Europe" (the economy, the market, and the currency, let's say) and what concerns the "national" level (let's say, the social and political pact) has been shaken once and for all. Today, the new economic policies conducted in the name of the "stability of the euro" affect taxation, national budgets, competitiveness, and "structural reforms" (labor market and such): in short, the core powers of national parliaments. It is hard to see how the European Parliament alone can decide on recommendations for the budgets of eurozone states, on the corporation tax base, on policies of economic and social convergence, and so forth. That would be to challenge the very foundation of democracy, which has rested taxation on the vote by representatives of the nation ever since 1215 and the Magna Carta. More: it would be to empty national democracies of their substance.

Rather than counterpose "the national" and "the European," the T-Dem bases itself on the political legitimacy and foothold of national parliaments, to construct the democratic framework where the policies of economic convergence and social and fiscal harmonization necessary for a good governance of the eurozone can be initiated. By making the national legislator a European legislator, it aims to bring what is at stake in European politics into the heart of national elections.

So why wish for a group of members of the European Parliament to make up one-fifth of the Assembly?

The proportions matter little at this stage and are, of course, open to discussion. The key thing to stress is the usefulness of a *hybrid* form of representation combining representatives of national parliaments and representatives of the European Parliament. The latter are not only inured to the logic of EU institutions; they also represent European citizens as a whole and, in this capacity, attend to a general European interest. They are therefore particularly well placed to verify the *European* objectives in the light of which the government of the euro area will attempt to coordinate national economic and budgetary policies; well placed, too, to draw up a eurozone budget in conformity with the community interest of eurozone states and so on.

In giving so many powers to this Parliamentary Assembly of the Euro Area, are you not creating an Assembly regime?

An Assembly regime? That criticism has been made with reference to the powers that the Parliamentary Assembly of the Euro Area would have vis-à-vis the Eurogroup. The term is, of course, pejorative: it relates to various political episodes in the history of France (the National Convention regime of 1792, the Third Republic), that are said to have conflated the executive and legislative powers to the profit of the latter.

But this involves a profound misunderstanding of what the "separation of powers" means in democratic theory. It has never meant that the executive power is autonomous—if that were so, we would lapse into a regime that might be called "autocratic." Rather, the "separation of powers" signifies a regime where the powers cooperate with each other and the functions of each are clearly identified: for example, a legislative power that defines the general rules of political society, and an executive power that takes actions applying those general rules.

The T-Dem follows this conception in full. The Parliamentary Assembly has a legislative and budgetary power and frames the conditions for the decision making of bodies that carry out executive tasks. For example, it participates in drawing up the agenda and work program of the executive bodies (Eurogroup, Euro Summits), but it never substitutes itself for them.

The aim of the T-Dem is precisely to react against this autocratic tendency, which was already pointed out by Jürgen Habermas. This is the reason the T-Dem gives the final say to the Parliamentary Assembly of the Euro Area in the legislative and budgetary procedure—it provides a way to also break with the current dominance of the intergovernmental logic, which, as we have seen, produced mainly blockages and the insuperable opposition of state interests.

Has the European Commission been sacrificed?

The main aim of the T-Dem is to create a euro-area Parliamentary Assembly as a counterweight to the present governance of the euro area. It therefore does not focus on the Commission, whose role in this new power system is already well defined. But nor does it reduce the Commission's powers: the Commission participates in all levels of the governance of the euro area; it takes part in Euro Summits (meetings of the heads of state and government), in meetings of the Eurogroup (meetings of finance ministries), and in meetings of its powerful preparatory committees (Economic Policy Committee and Economic and Financial Committee). It is therefore perfectly capable of asserting the community interest in those contexts. Indeed, through its presence in the Eurogroup, it can play its traditional role of giving legislative impetus and thereby participate to the new legislative and budgetary powers envisaged by the T-Dem.

But you are embarking on a federal leap!

"Federal leap" is what some have called it! They say that, in proposing a common budget and a pooling of debts above 60% of GDP, the T-Dem is falling for the dark side of European power. Well, now, the very composition of the Parliamentary Assembly invalidates that argument: it is not a *supranational* Assembly, but a transnational Assembly consisting of networked national parliamentarians who represent and horizontally associate national political forces.

"A retreat into sovereigntism, then," we might hear next! Not true either. For in this Assembly with real powers to define European economic, fiscal, and budgetary policies, there will certainly emerge transnational political divisions—divisions that not only are linked to national affiliations (as is the case today in the Eurogroup or the European Council) but also redraw the map of the European left and right.

If there is a leap, then, it is into "transnational politics." For it is precisely there that the governance of the euro area is today being constructed, at the intersection of "the national" (treasury directors, national central bankers, economics ministers, and such) and "the European" (European Central Bank directorate, Commission officials). We therefore need to rid ourselves of the binary oppositions (federalism / sover-eigntism) that are today an obstacle to the understanding of Europe *as it is;* and to work to build this bridge between the national demo-cratic forces that alone are capable of giving the European project a new direction.

What is the purpose of proposing a *treaty?*

First and foremost to get away from conventional discourse and incan-tatory rhetoric about "the future of Europe." But a further reason is that the treaty form has the same virtue that constitutions have at the national level: it enables us to examine in detail and highlight the place of each (notably, the sovereign people) within the architecture of European power. In so doing, it invites us to claim the seemingly technical issues of Europe's economic and monetary policies for ourselves—as in 2005 during the French referendum campaign on the European Constitution—by putting forward counterarguments and amendments. The T-Dem, then, is by no means a turnkey treaty or a "take it or leave it" text. Quite the contrary. It is a first draft, which proposes a reform orientation around which a task of collective composition can begin.

Is it not simply unrealistic?

In politics, particularly European politics, we should be wary of dis-missing things out of hand as unrealistic. European history in the last few decades proves that the boundaries of the possible and the impos-sible are peculiarly mobile. Faced with the political and economic crises that have punctuated the EU integration project, European leaders have not hesitated to rummage through the drawers again and to show proof of great inventiveness. What is most unrealistic in the present context of the "European project" is the status quo! To stick to that means thinking that the European project can break out of its present isola-tion through a kind of "surface democratization"—like the one proposed by the many expert committees that blossomed in Brussels over the past five years, which sees parliaments (national or European) as rubber-stamping chambers exercising at best a kind of retrospective account-ability, in accordance with an authorization model of democracy that is today in profound crisis. The most unrealistic approach, in short,

1688 HOW TO DEMOCRATIZE EUROPE

would be to leave the definition of European solutions to the extreme right-wing populist movements that have succeeded in imposing a *transnational* framework on the present crisis—one that speaks of a new national-centeredness, a rejection of solidarity, and a revival of intra-European rivalry.

What is your method?

Of course, there will be no change without a real power balance with the economic and political forces that wish to maintain the enclave of technocratic management of European policies. The only question is *on what terrain* to act out this balance of power and to force the necessary alliances for this *new European political compromise.*

As we know, some propose to construct this power balance on the terrain of the clash between states, by playing the game of ultimatums and unilateral disobedience. Whatever the importance of the states in question, be they "the whole" of Great Britain or France, there is a risk of getting into an opposition of "national sovereignty" against "national sovereignty." Without dwelling here on the dangers of a new period marked by bilateral reprisals and all-out fiscal and economic competition between states, we should say that this national-state strategy is doubtless not the one most capable of constructing a European reform-oriented alliance and developing the necessary political power balance. Besides, this national strategy of "taking back control" will not by itself conjure away a European level of power marked by strong economic, financial, bureaucratic, and juridical integration. That level will continue to exist and to exert its political, economic and social effects on France.

The T-Dem proposes a different strategy. Its aim is to build this new power balance on a terrain on which a much broader coalition of players can be constructed, one on which various players—governments, of course, but also political groups, trade unions, and community associations, as well as reformist segments of employers' circles and such—may have an interest in together creating the necessary room for maneuver within the European project. This is *the terrain of democracy:* the terrain that, facing the combined effects of financial markets and the technocratic temptation, puts the sovereignty of peoples back at the heart of

European politics, but that also makes it possible to forge new kinds of alliance around *concrete* projects and solutions for change.

—*Translated by Patrick Camiller*

Note

1. This text, which offers a fictional dialogue on the T-Dem proposal, was first published in earlier form on the blog "Doyolaw. Politique. Justice. Libertés," *Libération*, April 13, 2017.

European Parliamentary Sovereignty on the Shoulders of National Parliamentary Sovereignties

We are very grateful that the Verfassungsblog has been one of the very first forums engaging the discussion on the Treaty on the Democratization of the Governance of the Euro Area (T-Dem).[1] While the proposal has emerged in the framework of the current French presidential campaign, and is now widely debated in this context, it has been primarily thought of as a contribution to the ongoing transnational conversation over the future of the European Union. As authors of the proposal, we first wish to thank our colleague Sébastien Platon for launching an interesting discussion about the T-Dem. While he raises a number of points that we wish to respond to, in the hope of fostering what we believe, indeed, is a much-needed debate, we note that his blog post converges with our views that "something must be done to increase the democratic accountability of the governance of the euro area," a diagnosis that is indicative of a growing consensus across Europe—recently exemplified by commissioner and longtime member of the Eurogroup Pierre Moscovici, who acknowledged that such an informal body "cannot anymore take its decisions, decide on budgetary policy or on the future of Greece for example late in the night and in secret *(huis clos)*."

It is not the place here, in the short format of a blog post, to present all the political ins and outs of the T-Dem. A short book presenting these at more length is being published in France (Seuil, 2017) and translations will become available in the coming months in several European languages. Before coming to a more limited number of observations here (for more, see the chapter "Sur la faisabilité juridique d'un traité de démocratisation de la gouvernance de la zone euro," in Stéphanie Hennette, Thomas Piketty, Guillaume Sacriste, Antoine Vauchez, *Pour un traité de démocratisation de l'Europe* [Seuil, 2017]) and engaging with the arguments put forward by our colleague Sébastien Platon, we would like to make some caveats in order to set the stage for a constructive debate.

First of all, on the treaty format itself: our intention with this format is to bring to the fore a concrete proposal. It appeared to us that offering such proposal in the form of a "treaty" could be a way of escaping the ritual and often rhetorical oppositions that have too often hampered the debate over the future of the EU. It should be clear, however, that the T-Dem is not to be taken as a full-fledged or "prêt à porter" treaty, but instead as a starting point for discussion. As longtime observers and scholars of EU affairs, we are fully aware of the fact that any reformist strategy at the EU level evolves in a legal and political minefield. More often than not, new proposals meet up with a number of crossed vetoes that unfold along a variety national, political, and legal lines. While some of the solutions put forward in the T-Dem may appear unconventional to some EU studies specialists, we wish to acknowledge the fact that these solutions all have to be considered in the wider political and legal context of our time. It is hard to downplay the polymorphous crisis and current challenges that the European Union is now facing. It's no wonder that theories of disintegration have become a new trend, not only in academia but in the larger public as well. . . .

No Time to Lose

Hence, the T-Dem starts from the premise that we have little time ahead to redress the course of the European project. Because a full revision of the EU treaties seems to be out of reach, we suggest a democratic transplant right at the core of the existing system of governance of the euro area. For that reason, as indicated hereafter, the T-Dem is not a self-standing proposal but instead a democratic addition to the institutional setup that has chaotically emerged in the context of the euro-area crisis. In proceeding in this way, we have started from the premise that historically, the European Union has demonstrated impressive flexibility in finding new institutional arrangements when it has faced critical junctures (and the responses to the euro-area crisis are textbook examples in this regard). To a certain extent, the proposed T-Dem assumes that such flexibility can be used to address the current political emergency and to redirect the European project beyond the current alternative between Brussels's status quo and the nationalistic turn taken by some of our democracies.

First and foremost, we would like to illuminate the overall legal approach that we have taken as we worked on the T-Dem. As Sébastien Platon rightly insists, all efforts undertaken with a view to democratize the euro area need to "take into account the specific constraints arising from the EU legal framework." As we have worked toward the T-Dem, we have certainly been very well aware of this. In fact, this is precisely the reason we have chosen to propose a Treaty that, as much as it tries to run counter the substantial logic of both the European Stability Mechanism (ESM) and the Treaty on Stability, Coordination and Governance in the Economic and Monetary Union, walks the same technical path: that of an international treaty that the states can agree to sign and ratify in parallel to their EU commitments. As Sébastien Platon rightly recalls, the ESM Treaty's compatibility with EU Law has indeed been challenged before the CJEU. But as a matter of fact, it was upheld by the Court, in a decision that we believe is crucial in opening up venues for political and institutional margins of maneuver. In fact, the 2012 *Pringle* ruling by the Court is very much our point of departure, as it affirms, inter alia, that the ESM treaty did not affect common rules on economic and monetary policy (§101) and that, therefore, member states were not precluded from signing such an international treaty. It seems to us that this line of reasoning (on which states further rested as they also signed the TSCG) can be prolonged and applied to the T-Dem, which merely seeks to democratize the governance of the euro area and (unlike the ESM treaty) hardly affects the monetary exclusive competence of the EU.

To be sure, if member states retain the possibility of concluding international agreements in parallel to the EU, it is under the condition that these are "consistent with European Union law" (§109). Again, however, the T-Dem is very careful to preserve such consistency. The main innovation proposed by the T-Dem is the creation of a Parliamentary Assembly of the Euro Area, endowed with powers of legislation and political control. Because it seeks to affirm the Assembly as a democratic counterpart to the existing bodies that are involved in the governance of the euro area, and in particular to the Eurogroup, the T-Dem foresees that the Assembly shall participate to the preparation of the meetings of the Euro Summits, express its views on the Commission's Alert Mechanism Reports or the European Central Bank's annual reports and price stability objectives, or vote on the financial assistance facilities decided in accordance with article 13 of the EMS treaty. It shall also vote a budget for the euro area, and vote on the candidates chosen inter alia for the presidency of the Euro Group or the managing director of the European Stability Mechanism.

Given how we have set it up, we do not believe the T-Dem is inconsistent with EU law—not to mention that the T-Dem includes a provision stating that it "shall be applied and interpreted by the Contracting Parties in conformity with the Treaties on which the European Union is founded, in particular Article 4(3) of the Treaty on European Union, and with European Union law, including procedural law whenever the adoption of secondary legislation is required." The main reason it can be argued that the T-Dem is compatible with existing EU law has to do with the actual current legal standing of the governance of the euro area, much of which is the result of political and institutional answers to the Eurozone crisis more than it is the result of any particular treaty or, for that matter, any particular democratically grounded grand design.

The governance of the euro area today involves a polymorphous ensemble of institutions, of which some are EU institutions (the ECB, the Commission) and some are non-EU, including informal, institutions. In particular, it is important to keep in mind that the Eurogroup's existence is hardly acknowledged by the EU treaties (art. 137 of the TFEU merely mentions its existence and refers to the protocol on the Eurogroup, which itself foresees that "the Ministers of the member states whose currency is the euro shall meet informally"), whereas the Euro Summits are only explicitly foreseen in the TSCG. In other words, the very existence and role of critical actors of the governance of the euro area are mostly informal—and certainly nowhere to be found in EU treaties themselves. Consequently, because much of the democratic imbalances that it seeks to correct have taken root outside EU law, the T-Dem's claim of compatibility with EU law is strong indeed: the T-Dem does not alter the EU institutional or legal framework in any substantial way.

No Institutional Highjacking

We therefore need to disagree with the characterization that the T-Dem organizes the "highjacking" of "existing bodies of the EU." In line with the framework determined by the Court in the *Pringle* case, the T-Dem does not "alter the essential character of the powers conferred" on EU institutions (§158). Nor does it allow EU institutions to any new power to make decisions of their own (§161).

Maybe the highjacking argument could indeed be made if the TFEU did truly define the role of the Eurogroup; but it does not—and it matters greatly to the T-Dem that article 136 is really about the Council and not the Eurogroup. This is why the T-Dem may endow the Eurogroup (together with the Parliamentary Assembly of the Euro Area) with legislative powers without affecting its definition by EU treaties (because it is, essentially, nonexistent). Let us consider, for example, the field of fiscal harmonization, a critical domain that falls under the category of "shared competences" in which the EU has repeatedly failed to intervene: In the framework of the T-Dem, the Parliamentary Assembly of the Euro Area and the Eurogroup would jointly have the capacity to draft and adopt the much-needed bill in case the EU keeps refraining from doing so. We therefore argue that the T-Dem may very well focus much of its attention on the Eurogroup, and seek to rebalance the Eurogroup's powers and role in order to carve out some space for interventions of the new democratic body it creates (the Parliamentary Assembly) without running counter to the TFEU. It is along similar lines that we wish to rebut Platon's observation that the T-Dem runs counter article 14 of the TFEU: The T-Dem does not alter the legislative, budgetary, and political control functions of the European Parliament within the EU. These remain very much untouched by the T-Dem, which merely foresees that some members of the EP become members of the Parliamentary Assembly of the Euro Area—whose creation and existence, in parallel to the EU, does not affect any EU institution.

In other words, although Platon is obviously right in insisting that "even though the new structure is officially disconnected from the EU institutional system, it is obviously linked to it," we do not feel that this is a situation created by the proposed T-Dem. The situation as it exists today is already a situation in which the euro area exists and has its own system of governance—which, also, is "officially disconnected from the EU institutional system" although "obviously linked to it." The T-Dem does not create this situation but instead seeks to better it through democratic enhancement.

This latter observation also answers Platon's final observation that decisions taken by the bodies that take part in the governance of the euro area "would not become EU law." While very true, this again is not an innovation of the T-Dem but a mere consequence of a preexisting situation. In fact, the CJEU itself has already ruled that decisions taken by the Eurogroup are not "EU Law"—and has therefore rejected as inadmissible not only an application against a Eurogroup decision but also decisions by the Commission and the European Central Bank to the extent that they are decisions taken in the framework of the EMS and not the EU treaties (CJEU, Sept. 20, 2016, *Mallis and Malli v. Commission* and other cases C-106 / 15P). Consequently, despite the relevance of the question Sébastien Platon raises at the end of his post (What about the liability of member states for decisions taken within the euro area?), it is hardly an issue that is created by the T-Dem.

Democratizing the Euro Area

Sébastien Platon also seems to see the T-Dem as being based on "defiance of the European Parliament." We first wish to insist that the T-Dem proposes that one-fifth of the members of the Parliamentary Assembly of the Euro Area would be members of the European Parliament; and that several provisions of the T-Dem (such as art. 3(2)) insist that "[the Parliamentary Assembly] shall work in close cooperation with the European Parliament." Defiance toward the one truly democratic institution of the European Union is certainly not in order within the T-Dem, as the T-Dem itself seeks to enhance democracy. The T-Dem's realm, however, is democratization not of the EU itself but of the euro area. The T-Dem, therefore, is not proposed in defiance of the EP; instead, it respects the EP as an EU institution and merely seeks to associate it to the governance of the euro area.

In other words, there are both technical and political reasons for the T-Dem's proposal that four-fifths of the Parliamentary Assembly it creates be representatives of national parliaments and one-fifth be representatives of the European Parliament. The technical reason is precisely that the T-Dem does not alter the existence or competences of EU institutions—among which the EP plays a prominent role. The political reason is that the decisions and policies that are effectively taken in the framework of the euro-area governance (from the "European Semester" to the ESM conditionality mechanism) are very much intertwined with national policies and have a great impact at the national levels. In fact, the dramatic ways in which Greece's economic and social choices have been restricted by the management of the Greek debt crisis in 2015 precisely count as one of the most compelling examples that have convinced us—and many other European actors and citizens—that democratization had become both an emergency and a necessity. What the T-Dem really seeks to avoid, first of all, is the repetition of a situation in which any country of the euro area would be compelled to drastically lower the pensions or other benefits it serves, based merely on decisions taken by the governance of euro area that has emerged not so much from the EU treaties but from a combination of informal practices and their partial consolidation in treaties such as the EMS or the TSCG. Instead, what the T-Dem seeks to affirm is the necessary association of national democratic representatives to decisions taken in the realm of the euro area.

More generally, the T-Dem aims at creating the democratic institutional framework in which the necessary improvements of the governance of the euro area in terms of fiscal and social harmonization, budgetary capacity, and economic cooperation will be able to take place. If the governance of the euro area is to take these much-needed steps, it will necessarily enter the very core of national social and democratic pacts, thereby touching upon national parliaments' constitutional competences. Suffice it to mention the fact that taxes and budget have been—from the Magna Carta to the "no taxation without representation" principle of the first American colonies—integral to the formation of parliamentarism. Even those who were most hostile to the interference of national parliaments in EU affairs have now acknowledged the fact that the emerging veto power of national parliamentary assemblies in an increasing number of EU affairs (from the Bundestag's much-expected vote on the Greek bailout to the Wallon Parliament's position in the CETA trade agreements) is putting the whole governance of the European Union at risk of paralysis. Still, the T-Dem insists on including a share of MEPs in the Parliamentary Assembly of the Euro Area. This is not the place to discuss whether the proposed share is important enough; this is certainly a matter of discussion. Instead we would like to point out that a hybrid composition is necessary in order to ensure tight coordination with the EU as a whole and allow for a process of socialization of members of national parliaments to the European ethos, which is much needed in such a transnational political arena.

In other words, we certainly have no defiance toward the European Parliament as such. We simply believe that it is critical to "Europeanize" national parliament members and to make them work together with European Parliament members. To a large extent, our proposal is close in spirit to the view expressed by Joschka Fischer in his Berlin speech of May 12, 2000 (and again in his "Europeanizing Europe" op-ed of October 27, 2011). When, in 2000, Fischer proposed to create a European Chamber emanating from national parliaments (and composed of national parliament members) and argued that this would be a crucial step toward political union in Europe, no one in France—and particularly in the French left—bothered to answer. In a way, this is the failed dialogue that we are now pursuing; our proposed Assembly of the Euro Area (which could become a European Assembly if and when all EU countries adopt the euro) is close to the European Chamber advocated by Fischer. Like him, we believe that a genuine European parliamentary sovereignty needs to be built upon the shoulders of national parliamentary sovereignties, not against them.

To be sure, the T-Dem does not pretend to resolve all the pending technical issues—including that of the justiciability of the decisions taken within the euro area. Nor does it, for that matter, pretend to be fully implementable as such. The T-Dem is a proposal, and we are very grateful for the opportunity that the Verfassungsblog has started to grant us for discussing and hopefully bettering it.

Note

1. This text was initially published by the Verfassungsblog (VerfBlog, March 26, 2017) as a reply to a text by Sébastien Platon, "Democratizing the Euro Area without the European Parliament: Benoît Hamon's 'T-Dem'" (VerfBlog, March 13, 2017).

18

Europeanizing Politics, Politicizing Europe

After thanking Shahin Vallée and Laurent Warlouzet for their careful reading of our Draft Treaty on the Democratization of the Euro Area (T-Dem),[1] and prior to discussing their points of criticism, we should perhaps begin with a list of the pitfalls that threaten any discussion of the reform of euro-area policy. The terrain of European treaty reform is a genuine minefield, especially for those who wish to overcome the ritual opposition between "sovereignist" and "federalist" perspectives— as we sought to do with the T-Dem. Strongly tinged with expertise, the discussion often struggles to escape the barrage of reminders of legal, political, or economic unfeasibility, which often seems to override the axiological question as to the very direction of the European project.

The Space of European (Im)Possibilities

As interesting as they may be, the comments to which we would like to give some answers do not fully escape this slippery slope: Both S. Vallée and L. Warlouzet regard the T-Dem as essentially utopian. Thus, the treaty is said to have no chance of being accepted by a Germany that for sixty years has been entirely based on the independence of monetary policies and institutions. That an iconoclastic proposal like the T-Dem, launched from the academic field in the middle of the electoral campaign, has been taken up *in extenso* by European capitals no doubt does it great honor. And yet, one of the very real challenges in drafting this text was to demonstrate, contrary to the notion whereby the European Treaties mostly bring forth a space of *impossibility*, that there is indeed some leeway and latitude for a political refoundation. In this respect, the T-Dem takes a very serious view of the lessons taught by a decade of *ad hoc* treaties adopted outside the EU's sole institutional framework, of "conditionality policies" built at the limits of the mandates of euro-area institutions, and of acute conflicts of interpretation fought between constitutional courts over the founding treaties of the euro area—all of which have clearly shown that Europe is actually quite malleable, so long as the political will is there. The T-Dem specifically stresses that the old refrain of unfeasibility and the timid step-by-step political approach are out of date; it also seeks to highlight that, after the climax of the Greek crisis, the democratization of euro-area governance is nothing but the code name for the rescue plan that is needed by a political Europe caught up in the turmoil of a polycrisis with no historical precedent.

Beyond this, S. Vallée and L. Warlouzet essentially appear to criticize the T-Dem's options from a shared perspective that, for want of a better word, we might refer to as "communitarian." L. Warlouzet insists on the fact that the "democratic deficit," perceived specifically at the European level, is just as important as the weakness of national institutions, and that, under these conditions, a solution would involve "a more explicit politicization of the Commission." With even greater clarity, S. Vallée argues that "it is precisely because the European Commission lacks the budget and the necessary prerogatives to govern the single currency" that "euro-area governance" is so deficient; in this perspective, it would be necessary to centralize powers in the hands of the Commission, and thus to finally endow supranational institutions with the powers they need to impose themselves in the face of national political and economic egoisms. It is, therefore, clearly from the communitarian tradition that our commentators draw their inspiration when they link the resolution of the current political crisis of the Economic and Monetary Union to the reinforcement of a "European Parliament–European Commission" partnership, which would presumably be freed from the "contingencies of national politics and domestic parliamentary alliances" and capable, *consequently*, of serving the general European interest.

But here again, the T-Dem makes a different choice. Drawing on more than a decade of social science studies in the fields of political economy,[2] political science,[3] historical sociology,[4] and EU law,[5] our proposal follows from the scientifically grounded conviction that the European project has undergone a profound change since the Maastricht Treaty. As a result of monetary integration and the economic and financial crisis of the last decade, Europe is, in fact, no longer the same. So long as it was a question of creating and co-managing a common market, or of establishing environmental and health standards, Europe could function with its primitive "communitarian" architecture, which places the European Commission at the political forefront, under the control of the member states and the European Parliament.

But with the monetary union and the multiple coordination and monitoring policies built urgently to save the euro "whatever it takes," European policy has suddenly spread to the heart of state sovereignty. It no longer intervenes only in what has been defined in the Treaties as the Community domain (the economy, the market, the currency, competition), but also, well beyond this, in what constitutes the core of states' political and social pacts (social policies, labor law, the determination of budgets and, by the same token, the voting of taxes). In other words, it touches on the *raison d'être* of national parliaments as defined by the Magna Carta of 1215!

To this we can add another observation: A government of the euro area has gradually differentiated itself within the European Union; a center of power has formed around the central pole of the Eurogroup (i.e., in this informal venue that brings together the national economic and financial bureaucracies, the Commission, and the ECB), which has imposed itself in just a few years as one of the decisive sites wherein states' basic economic orientations are defined (privatization, labor market reform, level of pensions, etc.).[6]

Better yet, the crisis has demonstrated, via the asymmetric effects of monetary integration and the worsening of economic and social inequalities in the euro area, that the future of the nineteen member states depends on their ability to reorganize this "government" in depth: by endowing it with the capacity to invest in common public goods, to conduct fiscal and social harmonization, and to build solidarity through debt pooling—all levers without which the common currency is not viable, as we now know.

Placing Democracy Back at the Center of European Policies

For all these reasons, the T-Dem wishes, first and foremost, to take note of this new situation that has forced the euro area to enter the era of "shared competences," and to begin anew from the observation that there has taken place an unprecedented blurring of the demarcation between the "national" and the "European." In this context, rethinking European democracy means overcoming the now-paralyzing opposition between "national problems" and "European solutions." It also means reflecting on a democratic framework that would make it possible to legitimately debate and decide on the policies of fiscal and social harmonization, budgetary convergence, and economic cooperation that are necessary for the future development of the euro area.

The Treaty on the Democratization of the Euro Area thus proposes a democratic and pluralistic institutional framework for such a government. It calls for the creation of an *ad hoc* Assembly in charge of monitoring this government closely, which would be composed, for one-fifth of its members, of European parliamentarians, and, for four-fifths of its members, of national parliamentarians (T-Dem, arts. 2–4). It is unlikely that the traditional "communitarian" formula would be up to the task if it entrusted the European Parliament alone with the mission of defining the budgetary stance, economic priorities, and fiscal policies of the euro area. Beyond the very real risk that this would gradually deprive national parliaments of their basic powers, thus causing national democracies to be partly emptied of their substance, it must be said that the composition of the Parliamentary Assembly of the Euro Area would be more in line with a democratic theory which states that representatives of the citizens affected by political decisions must be in charge of discussing and taking these decisions. If a commission of the European Parliament were responsible for monitoring the Eurogroup, we would find ourselves in the awkward situation where the representatives of the 28 member states of the EU would participate in defining the policies and reforms envisaged in the 19 states of the euro area!

Thus, many have duly noted this new situation and come to believe that the creation of a parliament and budget of the euro area should be placed at the heart of the European reform agenda. The President of the French Republic and the European Commissioner for Economic and Financial Affairs are now apparently convinced of this—more so than they seemed to be five months ago, when this project was first drafted. And the idea is not absent in Germany—far from it. Its most active supporters are in Germany, from the current minister of state for Europe, Michael Roth (SPD),[7] to the former minister of foreign affairs, Joschka Fischer. Angela Merkel herself does not seem completely hostile to it—though she would probably need to be in a position to stop the intractable Schäuble from conducting European affairs.

Of course, it remains to be seen whether we can count, as the T-Dem does, on national parliaments to change the status quo in Brussels. We should not be blind to the specific difficulties that would likely arise from such an Assembly of national parliamentarians: How to organize European political work? How to avoid the repercussions of specialization around a small group of Assembly members? How to counteract the effects of European electoral asynchrony whereby parliaments are elected according to 19 different calendars? And so on. As valid as these issues may be, we see them less as objections (any European political project is ultimately affected by those dynamics) than as an invitation to continue to reflect on the practical conditions for such transnational parliamentarism. More fundamentally, the fact remains that "national parliamentarians as a whole," evoked by S. Vallée concerning the Parliamentary Assembly of the Euro Area, would be much more likely to wrest the Eurogroup from the notoriously opaque, ineffective, and asymmetric logic of national interests, and to integrate it into a transnational political dynamic. This is because this Assembly would take place under a regime of publicity and deliberation; it would be built with the parliamentary oppositions; and it would be goaded by members of the European Parliament (who would constitute one-fifth of the members of the Parliamentary Assembly of the Euro Area). Consequently, far from being intergovernmental, as S. Vallée claims, our solution bets on the ability of this Assembly to serve as a privileged place for European *demoi-cracy*—rooted in a plurality of national public spaces and able to finally bring forth the divisions, identities, and solidarities (that is, concrete public goods) that would draw the "European project" out of the isolation and diffuse indifference that effectively constitute the primary European challenge.

The Cost of the Status Quo

Finally, let us conclude with a question for our two detractors: What exactly do you propose, if not the defense of the status quo and of the current institutional equilibrium? After so much mistrust was expressed—referendum after referendum—toward European integration in the last twenty years, and after the Brexit vote revealed that the whole integration process could founder, inertia seems to us an indefensible position. Both S. Vallée and L. Warlouzet seem to share our dissatisfaction with the Eurogroup of finance ministers, with its opacity, with its growing influence over euro-area governance, and, above all, with its inability to take calm majority decisions after genuine public and democratic deliberation. But by what means do they propose to escape this equilibrium?

Without stating it explicitly, both seem to have in mind a model in which the Commission would regain control by mainly relying on the European Parliament, and by largely bypassing the Eurogroup. There are two problems with this view. First, the authors should have presented their solution more thoroughly. Our proposal can, of course, be criticized and improved, but it has at least the merit of being clear. In particular, our draft Treaty explicitly provides that in the event of disagreement between the Eurogroup and the Parliamentary Assembly of the Euro Area—especially concerning the vote on the euro-area budget—the Parliamentary Assembly would have the last word (T-Dem, arts.12–15). If S. Vallée proposes that the European Parliament in its current form should have the final say in the event of disagreement with the Eurogroup, then he should write it clearly. And if this is not what he proposes, and if in reality the Eurogroup should in his view retain its current blocking capacity, then the institutional status quo remains in place.

Second, and most importantly, if we genuinely wish to escape the current intergovernmental logic and the impasses of the Eurogroup, then it is essential, we believe, to fundamentally rethink the structure of European parliamentarism and to accord a central place to national parliamentarians. The reason is simple: In order to reduce the influence of national executives over European decisions, the key players in the game should naturally be the bodies on which the executives of the member states found their legitimacy—namely, national parliaments. Otherwise there can be no binding link between national democratic institutions and European ones, which seems neither realistic nor desirable. Our proposal would also contribute to the profound Europeanization of the political life of member states: In each national legislative election, parties and candidates would have to discuss their program of action for the Parliamentary Assembly of the Euro Area, and would no longer be able to merely deflect blame onto European institutions that presumably are free from of all control—or at least they would no longer be able to do so as easily as in the present system. Our proposition is no doubt imperfect and incomplete. Nevertheless, it seems to us salutary that the European institutional debate finally rests on specific proposals and counterproposals. This will make it possible to judge on results, and to find the best solutions together.

Notes

1. This text was written in September 2017 in reaction to comments published by Shahin Vallée and Laurent Warlouzet on *La vie des idées*. We wish to thank the editorial committee and the translator for their work. http://www.booksandideas.net/Politicizing-Europe-Europeanizing-Politics.html.
2. Michel Aglietta and Nicolas Leron, *La double démocratie* (Seuil, 2017).
3. See, in particular, Christopher Bickerton, *European Integration: From Nation-States to Member States* (Oxford: Oxford University Press, 2012); see also Uwe Puetter, *The Eurogroup: How a Secretive Circle of Finance Ministers Shape European Economic Governance* (Manchester: Manchester University Press, 2006).
4. See Kenneth Dyson, *States, Debt, Power* (Oxford: Oxford University Press, 2014), and Wolfgang Streeck, *Buying Time: The Delayed Crisis of Democratic Capitalism* (London: Verso, 2014); see also, from a different political perspective that nonetheless shares many elements of this diagnosis, the Habermasian critique of the "post-democratic autocracy" formed by the euro-area government.
5. Mark Dawson, Henrik Enderlein, and Christian Joerges, eds., *Beyond the Crisis: The Governance of Europe's Economic, Political and Legal Transformation* (Oxford: Oxford University Press, 2015).
6. See the unflattering descriptions of the Eurogroup made by Pierre Moscovici in numerous interventions.
7. Michael Roth, "Der Euro braucht ein Parlament: Für eine Avantgarde von Demokratie und Solidarität," *Friedrich Ebert Stiftung* (November 2011).

19

Manifesto for the Democratization of Europe

MANON BOUJU, LUCAS CHANCEL, ANNE-LAURE DELATTE,
STÉPHANIE HENNETTE, THOMAS PIKETTY, GUILLAUME
SACRISTE, ANTOINE VAUCHEZ

We, European citizens, from different backgrounds and countries, are today launching this appeal for the in-depth transformation of European institutions and policies. This Manifesto contains concrete proposals—in particular, a project for a Democratization Treaty and a Budget Project that can be adopted and applied as it stands by the countries who so wish, with no single country being able to block those who want to advance. It can be signed online (www.tdem.eu) by all European citizens who identify with it. It can be amended and improved by any political movement.

Following Brexit and the election of anti-European governments at the head of several member countries, it is no longer possible to continue as before. We cannot simply wait for the next departures, or further dismantling, without making fundamental changes to present-day Europe.

Today, our continent is caught between rival political movements. On the one hand are movements whose programme is confined to hunting down foreigners and refugees, a programme they have now begun to put into action. On the other hand we have parties that claim to be European but in reality continue to hold that hard-core liberalism and the spread of competition to all (states, firms, territories, and individuals) are enough to define a political project. They in no way recognize that it is precisely this lack of social ambition that leads to the feeling of abandonment.

There are some social and political movements that do attempt to end this fatal dialogue by moving in the direction of a new political, social, and environmental foundation for Europe. After a decade of economic crisis, there is no lack of these specifically European critical situations: structural underinvestment in the public sector, particularly in the fields of training and research; a rise in social inequality; acceleration of global warming; and a crisis in the reception of migrants and refugees. But these movements often find it difficult to formulate an alternative project or to describe precisely how they would like to organize the Europe of the future and the decision-making infrastructure specific to it.

We, European citizens, by publishing this Manifesto, Treaty, and Budget, are making specific proposals publicly available to all. These proposals are not perfect, but they do have the merit of existing. The public can access them and improve them. They are based on a simple conviction: Europe must build an original model to ensure the fair and lasting social development of its citizens. The only way to convince them is to abandon vague and theoretical promises. If Europe wants to restore solidarity with its citizens, it can only do so by providing concrete proof that it is capable of establishing cooperation between Europeans and by making those who have gained from globalization contribute to the financing of the public goods that are cruelly lacking in Europe today. This means making large firms contribute more than small and medium businesses, and making the richest pay more taxes than poorer taxpayers. This is not the case today.

Our proposals are based on the creation of a Budget for democratization that would be debated and voted by a sovereign European Assembly. This will at last enable Europe to equip itself with a public institution that is both capable of dealing with crises in Europe immediately and able to produce a set of fundamental public and social goods and services in the framework of a lasting and solidarity-based economy. In this way, the promise, made as far back as the Treaty of Rome, of "improving living and working conditions" will finally become meaningful.

This Budget, if the European Assembly so desires, will be financed by four major European taxes, the tangible markers of this European solidarity. These will apply to the profits of major firms, the top incomes (over 200,000 euros per annum), the highest wealth owners (over 1 million euros), and carbon emissions (with a minimum price of 30 euros per tonne). If it is fixed at 4% of GDP, as we propose, this budget could finance research, training, and the European universities, an ambitious investment program to transform our model of economic growth, the financing of the reception and integration of migrants, and the support of those involved in operating the transformation. It could also give some budgetary leeway to member states to reduce the regressive taxation that weighs on salaries or consumption.

The issue here is not to create a "transfer payments Europe" that would endeavor to take money from the "virtuous" countries to give it to those who are less so. The project for a Treaty of Democratization (www.tdem.eu) states this explicitly by limiting the gap between expenditure deducted and income paid by a country to a threshold of 0.1% of its GDP. This threshold can be raised in case there is a consensus to do so, but the real issue is elsewhere: it is primarily a question of reducing the inequality within the different countries and of investing in the future of all Europeans—beginning, of course, with the youngest among them, with no single country having preference. This computation does exclude spending that benefits all countries equally, such as policies to curb global warming. Because it will finance European public goods benefiting all countries, the Budget for democratization will de facto also foster convergence between countries.

Because we must act quickly but must also get Europe out of the present technocratic impasse, we propose the creation of a European Assembly. This will enable these new European taxes and the budget for democratization to be debated and voted on. This European Assembly can be created without changing the existing European treaties.

This European Assembly would, of course, have to communicate with the present decision-making institutions (in particular the Eurogroup, in which the ministers for finance in the eurozone meet informally every month). But in cases of disagreement, the Assembly would have the final word. If not, its capacity to be a locus for a new transnational, political space where parties, social movements, and NGOs would finally be able to express themselves, would be compromised. Its actual effectiveness would equally be at stake, since the issue is one of finally extricating Europe from the eternal inertia of intergovernmental negotiations. We should bear in mind that the rule of fiscal unanimity in force in the European Union has for years blocked the adoption of any European tax and sustains the eternal evasion into fiscal dumping by the rich and the most mobile, a practice that continues to this day despite all the speeches. This will go on if other decision-making rules are not set up.

Given that this European Assembly will have the ability to adopt taxes and to enter the very core of the democratic, fiscal, and social compact of member states, it is important to truly involve national and European parliamentarians. By granting national elected members a central role, the national parliamentary elections will de facto be transformed into European elections. National elected members will no longer be able to simply shift responsibility onto Brussels and will have no other option than to explain to the voters the projects and budgets that they intend to defend in the European Assembly. By bringing together the national and European parliamentarians in one single Assembly, habits of co-governance will be created which at the moment only exist between heads of state and ministers of finance.

This is why we propose, in the Democratization Treaty available online (www.tdem.eu), that 80% of the members of the European Assembly should be members of the national parliaments of the countries that sign the Treaty (in proportion to the population of the countries and the political groups), and 20% from the present European Parliament (in proportion to the political groups). This choice merits further discussion. In particular, our project could also function with a lower proportion of national parliamentarians (for instance, 50%). But in our opinion, an excessive reduction of this proportion might detract from the legitimacy of the European Assembly in involving all European citizens in the direction of a new social and fiscal pact, and conflicts of democratic legitimacy between national and European elections could rapidly undermine the project.

We now have to act quickly. While it would be desirable for all the European Union countries to join in this project without delay, and while it would be preferable that the four largest countries in the eurozone (which together represent over 70% of the GNP and the population in the zone) adopt it at the outset, the project in its totality has been designed for it to be legally and economically adopted and applied by any subset of countries who wish to do so. This point is important because it enables countries and political movements who so desire to demonstrate their willingness to make very specific progress by adopting this project, or an improved version, right now. We call on every man and woman to assume his or her responsibilities and participate in a detailed and constructive discussion for the future of Europe.

Note

A version of this Manifesto was published on December 9, 2018, in nine European daily newspapers—*Der Stantard, Die Welt, The Guardian, Le Monde, Le Soir, Politiken, Publico, Repubblica,* and *Vanguardia.*

– *Glossary* –

The difficulty in structuring the public debate on European economic policies does not only derive from the technical sophistication of the issues at stake. It also relates to the administrative multiplication of the policies and programs, and the legal entanglement of the many existing institutions and procedures. Over the years, a complex Euro-jargon has emerged, made out of countless bureaucratic syntagms and acronyms, which only few people, even among those directly concerned, can make sense of. As a direct consequence of such structural bias, citizens lack a proper understanding of the actual policies that are being conducted under this new governance framework, and a meaningful public debate about these policies is therefore being hindered. This glossary stands as a modest attempt to address such bias.

Broad Economic Policy Guidelines (BEPGs): Since their creation in 1997, these have provided the central framework for the coordination and surveillance of national economic policies. Each year, the Economic and Financial Affairs Council (the ECOFIN Council) adopts, on a proposal from the European Commission (EC), "economic policy guidelines recommendations," which are addressed to the member states of the EU and regard budgetary policy, structural reforms, wage setting, sustainable development policy, and so on. Since the launch of the European Semester in 2011, macroeconomic surveillance has been strengthened by the creation of a new Macroeconomic Imbalance Procedure (MIP). On the basis of a scoreboard for 10 indicators, the Commission screens macroeconomic developments in the member states and publishes an Alert Mechanism Report (AMR). Where deemed appropriate, it recommends that the ECOFIN Council open an Excessive Imbalance Procedure

(EIP). This recommends corrective measures to be adopted by the member state concerned (corrective action plan), and may, in case of repeated imbalances, impose financial sanctions (which may amount to up to 0.1% of the member state's GDP).

Directorates-General (DG): The Directorates-General are the main administrative units within the European Commission. The most relevant for the governance of the euro area are the DG ECFIN, which deals with economic and financial affairs; the DG EMPL, which is in charge of employment policy, social affairs, and inclusion; and the DG TAXUD, which focuses on taxation and customs union.

ECOFIN Council: The Economic and Financial Affairs Council is the section of the Council of the European Union responsible for EU policy in three main areas: economic policy, taxation issues, and the regulation of financial services. It is made up of the economics and finance ministers from all 28 member states, who meet up at least once a month. Its meetings and proceedings are prepared for by the Economic and Financial Committee (EFC).

Economic and Financial Committee (EFC): The EFC is probably the most powerful administrative body within the Council of the European Union. As an advisory organ established to facilitate the coordination of national economic and financial policies, it plays a crucial role in preparing the deliberations of the ECOFIN Council. It is composed of senior officials from national administrations (generally, Treasury directors) and central banks, the European Central Bank (ECB), and the Commission. The EFC also meets in a euro-area-specific formation, in which only the euro-area member states, the Commission, and the ECB participate. Under this format, the EFC prepares the deliberations of the Eurogroup.

Eurogroup: The Eurogroup is an informal body where finance ministers of the euro area discuss "questions related to the specific responsibilities they share with regard to the single currency." It focuses on matters pertaining to the budgetary, monetary, and structural policies of the euro-area countries. It holds preliminary discussions on the decisions of the ECOFIN Council and deliberates on the modalities financial assistance granted by the European Stability Mechanism (ESM) to euro-area countries experiencing serious financial difficulties. So far, those participating to Eurogroup meetings have most generally been the finance ministers of the euro area, the president of the Eurogroup (elected for two and a half years by the members of the Eurogroup), the vice president of the Commission for Economic and Monetary Affairs and the Euro, and the president of the European Central Bank. Its meetings and proceedings are prepared for by the Eurogroup Working Group (EWG).

Euro Summit: This is the highest decision-making body within the governance of the euro area. It was established in 2008 on a joint initiative of Angela Merkel and Nicolas Sarkozy in order to tackle the economic and financial crisis that confronted the euro area. The Summit brings together the heads of state and government of member states whose currency is the euro, and the president of the European Commission. Currently outside the Treaty framework, it defines the strategic orientations that are to guarantee the proper functioning of the euro area. Euro Summit meetings are convened by its president and take place at least twice a year in Brussels, but since the eurozone crisis unfolded, the number of extraordinary meetings has dramatically increased. These meetings produce statements summarizing common positions and action lines, which are adopted by consensus.

Eurogroup Working Group (EWG): Created in 2004, the EWG is the "euro-area" format of the Economic and Financial Committee (EFC). In a similar fashion, it is composed of senior officials from national finance ministries and central banks (of the euro-area member states) and representatives from the DG ECFIN and the ECB. It particularly focuses on the preparation of Eurogroup meetings and the management of this body.

European Employment Strategy (EES): The EES dates back to 1997 when EU member states first decided to agree on a set of common (nonbinding) objectives in the field of employment policy. From March 2000 onward, and since the Lisbon European Council, these priorities have been merged within the wider framework of the Broad Economic Policy Guidelines (BEPGs), with the declared objective of "strengthening employment, economic reform and social cohesion as part of a knowledge-based economy." Better known as the Lisbon Strategy, this coordination mechanism for national economic, social, and environmental policies is currently being continued in the framework of the Europe 2020 strategy for growth. In between, it has been integrated within the general framework for multilateral surveillance and coordination set up under the European Semester.

European Semester: So named because the process is mainly carried out over the first six months of each year, the European Semester is a cycle of coordination of national economic and budgetary policies, carried out under the auspices of the Commission and the Council. This cycle revolves around three axes: structural reforms, budgetary policies, and the sustainability of national public finances in accordance with the

Stability and Growth Pact (SGP), and the prevention of macroeconomic imbalances.

European Stability Mechanism (ESM): The ESM is the European financial assistance mechanism set up in 2012 by euro-area member states in order to address the risk of sovereign default in the area. It is run by a Board of Governors, bringing together the finance ministers of euro-area member states, and chaired by the president of the Eurogroup. Endowed with a total lending capacity of EUR 500 billion, and an authorized capital stock of EUR 702 billion, the ESM grants financial assistance ("stability support") in the form of loans, through the opening of precautionary credit lines, or by directly supporting the recapitalization of financial institutions. The ESM and the beneficiary member state sign a Memorandum of Understanding (MoU), which details the macroeconomic conditionality attached to the assistance—that is, a set of measures designed to stabilize the beneficiary state's public finances.

European Treaties: The European Union, which is currently still made up of 28 member states, is governed by two founding treaties, which are the result of a continued revision process:

- The Treaty on the Functioning of the European Union (TFEU), the successor of the Treaty establishing the European Economic Community, concluded in Rome in 1957, and subsequently amended by the Single European Act (1986), the Maastricht Treaty (1992), the Amsterdam Treaty (1997), the Nice Treaty (2001), and the Lisbon Treaty (2007).
- The Treaty on European Union (TEU) is a shorter instrument, which was set up by the Maastricht Treaty in 1992 and later amended by the Amsterdam (1997), Nice (2001), and Lisbon (2007) treaties.

Excessive Deficit Procedure (EDP): Initially defined by the Maastricht Treaty, the Excessive Deficit Procedure was integrated in 1997 into the broader framework of the Stability and Growth Pact in 1997 as its so-called corrective arm. When it appears, from the stability or convergence programs submitted by national authorities, and from the statistical analyses carried out by the Commission, that a member state runs a deficit deemed excessive or at risk of becoming excessive (the threshold being set at 3% GDP), the Commission prepares a report on the situation. It is for the ECOFIN Council to decide, after considering the observations from the member state concerned, whether an excessive deficit exists, and to trigger the corrective procedure. The Six-Pack has further strengthened the conditions under which a noncompliant member state under an Excessive Deficit Procedure may be punished: financial sanctions (which may consist in a fine amounting to from 0.2% up to

0.5% of the state's GDP) may only be avoided if opposed by a qualified majority within the Council ("reverse qualified majority" voting).

Six-Pack and Two-Pack: The Six-Pack and the Two-Pack are legislative packages adopted, respectively, in 2011 and 2013. Complemented in 2012 by the Treaty on Stability, Coordination and Governance (TSCG), better known as the European Fiscal Compact, they subject national economic and budgetary policies to a tight system of supervision, with the aim of strengthening compliance with the rules of the Stability and Growth Pact (1997) and the "Maastricht criteria" (1992). Bringing together all economic and budgetary policy coordination procedures under the European Semester framework, they enable the activation of the Excessive Deficit Procedure against member states whose debt ratio either exceeds the 60% GDP threshold or does not diminish at a satisfactory pace. The Six-Pack and Two-Pack introduce the possibility of progressive financial sanctions against noncompliant member states (up to 0.5% GDP), which shall be applied automatically (unless the Council objects by a qualified majority vote).

Stability and Growth Pact (SGP): The Stability and Growth Pact is a set of rules adopted in 1997 in order to coordinate national budgetary policies and to guarantee the soundness of national public finances. The Pact now consists of a preventive arm revolving around the achievement of a medium-term budgetary objective specific to each member state. It also includes a corrective arm, which is designed to ensure that member states adopt corrective actions if their public deficit or debt level exceeds the reference values set by the well-known "Maastricht criteria" (consecrated in the homonymous1992 Treaty) at 3% GDP for public deficit and 60% GDP for public debt.

Treaty on Stability, Coordination and Governance (TSCG): Better known as the European Fiscal Compact, the TSCG is an international treaty adopted in 2012 that imposes on euro-area member states (and on other EU member states that are willing to accede to the treaty) a common fiscal discipline by requiring them to consecrate in their national legal order the so-called golden rule (the balanced-budget principle). It further strengthens an already thick rulebook on budgetary convergence, made up of the "Maastricht criteria" (1992), the Stability and Growth Pact (1997), the Six-Pack (2011), and Two-Pack (2013).

Troïka: At the European level, the Troika is the tripartite administrative body jointly established by the European Commission, the European Central Bank, and the International Monetary Fund (IMF) to supervise the rescue plans and their implementation in EU member states (Cyprus, Spain, Greece, Portugal, Ireland).

—*Translated by Paul Dermine*

– *Contributors* –

Jeremy Adelman is the Director of the Global History Lab at Princeton University.

Vestert Borger is assistant professor in European law at Leiden University.

Manon Bouju is an economist.

Lucas Chancel is an economist and co-director of the World Inequality Lab at the Paris School of Economics

Anne-Laure Delatte is a CNRS Research professor and the deputy Director of CEPII.

Stéphanie Hennette is a professor at the Law School of the Université Paris–Nanterre.

Christian Joerges is a professor of Law and Society at the Hertie School of Governance Berlin and co-Director of the Centre of European Law and Politics at the University of Bremen.

Iphigénie Kamtsidou is a professor at the Law School of AUTH and President of the Centre national pour l'administration publique et territoriale.

Ulrike Liebert is a professor at the Jean Monnet Center for European Studies at the University of Bremen.

Paul Magnette professor of political science at the Université libre de Bruxelles (ULB), mayor of Charleroi and former minister in Belgium.

Pierre Moscovici is currently commissioner for economic and financial affairs, European Commission.

Kalypso Nicolaidis is a professor of international relations at the University of Oxford.

Thomas Piketty is a professor at the Paris School of Economics and a directeur d'études at the École des hautes études en sciences sociales.

Guillaume Sacriste is a professor of political science at the Université Paris 1–Sorbonne.

Rui Tavares is a researcher at the Centre for International Studies University Institute (Lisbon) and at the School of Transnational Governance, European University Institute (Florence).

Luuk van Middelaar is a professor at Leiden University.

Antoine Vauchez is a CNRS research professor in political science at the Université Paris 1–Sorbonne.

— *Index* —

Labor law, 128
Labor markets, 32
LABREF database, 32
Lacey, J., 103
Lacroix, J., 106
Laissez-faire, 126
Lampedusa, Giuseppe Tomasi di, 152
Lavenex, S., 103
Law: governance by, 103–104; international public law, 131; soft law, 131
Law, EU: Eurogroup decisions and, 175; primacy of, 145; T-Dem and, 84–85, 86, 172–173
Lebaron, F., 39, 40
Legislation: done by ambassadors, 155; Eurogroup and, 79–81; European Parliament and, 81; fundamental hierarchy in, 136; Six-Pack, 2, 23, 51, 63; in T-Dem, 64, 78–81, 82, 84, 98, 132–133; Two-Pack, 2, 23, 51, 63
Legislative initiative, powers of, 133
Legitimacy, 143; deficit of, decision making and, 109; of EMU, 103; of EU, 101; of Eurogroup, 112; of European institutions, 131; of IMF, 104; input, 150; of national parliaments, 164; output, 150; Parliamentary Assembly and, 144; resetting, 89 (*see also* Constituent moment); sources of, 100, 101
Lemoine, B., 39
Liberal economic ordering, destruction of, 126
LIME (Lisbon Methodology), 32
Lindseth, P. L., 103
Lisbon strategy, 32
Lisbon Treaty, 17, 51, 66, 67, 71, 132, 141, 142–143, 144, 145
Lupo, Nicola, 40

Maas, Cees, 16
Maastricht convergence criteria, 22, 29, 38
Maastricht Treaty, 15, 22, 23, 33, 40, 116, 124
Macroeconomic Imbalance Procedure (MIP), 23–24, 104
Macron, Emmanuel, x, 29, 115, 138
Maes, I., 39
Magna Carta, 180
Mallis and Malli v Commission, 175
Konstantinos Mallis v Commission and BCE, 49
Malta, 153

Manifesto for the Democratization of Europe, xi–xii, 185–189
Marcussen, M., 39
McNamara, K. R., 106
Meetings, 17
Member states: anti-European governments in, 185; credibility of, 29; economic policies and, 49; equality and political dignity and, 122; governments' dual responsibility in, 100; labor-law issues and, 128; reorganization of national administrations, 31; shared competences with EU, 79; Social Democratic governments, 32; surveillance of, 21; willingness to sign treaties, 152–153. *See also* European Union (EU); Parliaments, national
Memorandums of understanding (MoUs), 2, 18, 24–27, 31, 34, 118, 122. *See also* Financial assistance; Sovereign debt crisis
Merkel, A., 123, 182
Mersch, Yves, 16
Migrant crisis, 89, 92. *See also* Crises
Milleron, Jean-Claude, 14
Mingasson, Jean-Paul, 14
Ministers. *See* Eurogroup; Finance ministries
MIP (Macroeconomic Imbalance Procedure), 23–24, 104
Mitterrand, F., 13
Monetary Committee, 12–13, 15, 38
Monetary policy, 15. *See also* Economic and fiscal coordination/integration; Policies, economic; Stability
Monitoring. *See* Surveillance
Moravcsik, A., 39, 106
Moscovici, Pierre, 19, 36, 162
Mourlon-Druol, E., 39
Mudge, S., 40
Müller, Jan-Werner, 20

National interests, 113–114. *See also* Sovereignty, national
National life, liberty to organize, 126, 127. *See also* Sovereignty, national
Nazism, 126
Nicolaidis, K., 102, 103, 104, 105, 106
Norms, shared, 28

Officials, 28. *See also* Parliaments, national
Ohnmacht des Sollens (Hegel), 126